MARK

TRUSTING KING JESUS
AS THE ONE WHO SEES
YOU, SAVES YOU,
AND NEVER LETS GO

Written by Felicia Caid Smith | Designed by Anna Twumasi

All Scripture quotations are **English Standard Version (ESV)** unless otherwise noted.

We must exchange whispers with God before shouts with the world.

Lysa TerKeurst

PAIR YOUR STUDY GUIDE WITH THE FIRST 5 MOBILE APP!

This study guide is designed to accompany your study of Scripture in the First 5 mobile app. You can use it as a standalone study or as an accompanying guide to the daily content within First 5.

First 5 is a free mobile app developed by Proverbs 31 Ministries to transform your daily time with God.

Scan the QR code to download the First 5 app on your smartphone, and create a free account!

WWW.FIRST5.ORG

WELCOME TO MARK

Last spring, I joined a small group of women to study the book of Mark. When we first gathered at a local coffee shop with our Bibles open, I was confident I knew these scriptures well. The story was familiar to me. Yet somehow, as we studied the text and discussed it week after week, my heart received the gospel in a fresh and unexpected way.

This time around, reading Mark's words about Jesus felt like spending time with a lifelong friend and somehow getting to know Him even better. Have you ever done that?

When I was in college, I studied abroad with a friend I had known for years. I thought I knew her well before, as we had gone to school together since kindergarten, commuted to our college classes together every day, and even worked together. But that summer in Paris, while sharing a dorm room (without air conditioning) that measured 172 square feet including the bathroom ... we got to know each other on a whole new level.

The book of Mark invites us to know Jesus better than ever before. We will follow along on His journey from Galilee to the Decapolis and into Judea, then finally to the cross and the tomb. All the while, we'll discover how Mark puts the spotlight on King Jesus, the One who healed the sick, calmed storms, cast out demons, fed multitudes, befriended sinners, walked on water, hung on the cross, and rose from the dead.

With this powerful Savior in mind, at that very first small group meetup when I recently studied Mark, we gathered around a woman who was facing health challenges and prayed for her healing. I tried to pray mightily over her. I wanted to have bold faith!

But I'm going to be real with you ... Doubt crept into my prayers as I asked the Lord to remove what the doctors had diagnosed. In that moment, her medical problem felt enormous.

But as I studied the pages of Mark alongside my friends, I rediscovered a truth I should have never let slip away: No problem is too big for Jesus. Not blindness, bleeding, leprosy, paralysis, deformities, deafness ... not confusion, unbelief, oppression, corruption, or dark powers ... not even death. He does impossible things! Now, I remind my heart of His limitless power when I pray.

As we study Mark together, whether it's your first time or 50th time, I want to encourage you to get to know Jesus a little better. Knowing Him better changes *us* for the better. It gives us a better grip on the healing hem of His garment, like the woman we'll meet in Mark 5 — and as we hold on tight to our Savior, we find He is holding on to us. He's the One who never lets go.

My prayer, now a much bolder prayer, is that as you do this study, you will grow in the grace and knowledge of Jesus Christ. May He transform the way you pray, worship, fellowship, testify, serve, give, and live.

Your sister in Christ,

Felicia Caid Smith

To learn more about Felicia and how to connect with her, see Page 166.

WHAT KIND OF BOOK IS MARK?

THE "GOSPEL" AS A GENRE

If you walk into any major bookstore, you will likely see a biography section filled with books about the lives of notable people, from Abigail Adams to Madonna to Zhuang Zhou. Some of these stories inspire us, some serve as cautionary tales, and some are purely educational.

The book of Mark is a biography of Jesus Christ. But it cannot be categorized as *merely a biography.* For one thing, a considerable portion of the story takes place during Jesus' final week on earth, and many particulars of His early life (parentage, birth, childhood, education, and family) are noticeably absent.[1] Some of the text is also out of chronological order, not because Mark misremembered the timeline but because he had a particular, God-inspired focus for his writing. An important clue lies in the book's opening sentence: The author did not introduce this book as an account of *all* that Jesus said or did but rather as *"the gospel of Jesus Christ, the Son of God"* (Mark 1:1).[2]

In Mark's time and culture, the term "gospel," or *euangeliou* in Greek, meaning "good news," was used for proclamations of victory in battle or when announcing a significant event in the life of a Roman emperor. But in Mark 1:1, "*the gospel*" refers to Jesus' life, words, deeds, death, and resurrection — and what all this means for God's Kingdom and His plan to save us.[3] The book of Mark testifies about Jesus with the intent to lead people to know and follow Jesus; therefore, it may also be fitting to call it a "witness document." It was the first of what would become a new genre of literature: a "Gospel."[4]

HOW TO READ A GOSPEL

Even though the biblical Gospels (Matthew, Mark, Luke, and John) are not biographies in the modern sense, they share some similarities with ancient biographies, which recorded true facts about historical people but also had morals to their stories and presented certain characters as positive or negative examples. Some scholars have called the Gospels "Christological biographies" because they tell true stories about Jesus for the purpose of communicating theological truths that readers should know.[5] As we've already said, the Gospels are not *merely* biographies but also life-saving revelation from God. John puts it like this: "*These are written so that you may believe that Jesus is the Christ, the Son of God, and that by believing you may have life in his name*" (John 20:31).

At the same time, as we study the Gospels, it's wise to remember that the Bible was written *for* us but not necessarily *to* us. The Gospel of Mark was originally written to a first-century audience, and even before Jesus' words were recorded in this Gospel, He spoke them to specific ancient audiences some 30 years earlier. Sometimes Jesus spoke to Jews and other times to gentiles (non-Jews). Sometimes He addressed religious leaders and other times His disciples. To discover how Jesus' teachings apply to us today, we should first seek to understand what they meant to His original audience.[6] Scholars Duvall and Hayes write: "If we come up with a point that Jesus' audience would not grasp, we have probably missed the point."[7]

Don't worry — we don't have to become overnight experts on ancient Roman and Hebrew culture. But as we read the Gospel of Mark, we can do our best to seek understanding and put ourselves in the place of its first hearers, listening carefully and letting Jesus' words strike us the way they would have struck His original audience. Then we can better draw out timeless biblical principles that were relevant to first-century listeners and remain relevant to us as Christians today.

WHO WROTE
THE GOSPEL OF MARK?

Sometimes schoolteachers become detectives when they are grading assignments and come across a paper without a name written on it. To figure out whose work it is, they may begin with a process of elimination, ruling out whose it *is not*. If that doesn't prove successful, they may look for clues in the handwriting or the quality and content of the work. Sometimes they may just ask the class, "Does anyone recognize this paper?"

The Gospel of Mark did not originally have a name written on it either. In fact, all four Gospels are technically anonymous, and identifying the author from the text alone can be a challenge. Early manuscripts refer to "The Gospel of Mark" or "The Gospel According to Mark," but scholars believe these titles were added only after multiple Gospels were circulating together and specificity of authorship became necessary.[1]

Despite its anonymity, the Church has attributed authorship of this Gospel to Mark since the turn of the second century. Papias, a bishop in Asia Minor until about A.D. 130, was the earliest known writer to identify Mark as the author.[2] Although Papias did not know Jesus' apostles personally, he had direct contact with those who did and was privy to information about Mark's Gospel.[3] Papias' statement on the Gospel of Mark, as documented in Eusebius' *Historia Ecclesiastica (History of the Church)*, explains that Mark was not necessarily an eyewitness to Jesus' life and ministry, but he was close with the Apostle Peter and likely recorded Peter's account.[4]

You may know Peter as the disciple who walked on water with Jesus (Matthew 14:28-31), cut off a soldier's ear at Jesus' arrest (John 18:10; Mark 14:47), and denied Jesus three times (Mark 14:66-72). He was also the apostle who preached at Pentecost in Acts 2 and who opened the gospel to the gentiles in Acts 10-11. Papias suggests that Mark's Gospel relied on Peter's firsthand testimony and recollections of these events and more.

There is also a possibility that Mark himself personally witnessed some events in Jesus' ministry. Early Church tradition often identifies Mark as the young man in Mark 14:51-52 who was present at Jesus' arrest and wearing only a linen cloth, which he left behind when he fled the scene. If this is true, Mark may have had at least some firsthand encounters with Jesus.

What else do we know about Mark? Well, from the rest of the New Testament, we know he was sometimes called John Mark and was part of the Church from the very beginning. His mother, Mary, opened her home as a meeting place for Jesus' apostles in Acts 12:12, and Mark's cousin Barnabas was a faithful believer and apostle himself (Colossians 4:10; Acts 4:36).[5]

Barnabas traveled and taught alongside the Apostle Paul, and Mark accompanied them as an assistant or a kind of "ministry understudy" on their first missionary journey. But for reasons not recorded in Scripture, he departed early and returned to Jerusalem (Acts 13:13). Because Mark *"had not gone with them to the work,"* Paul later did not want to bring him along on a second missionary journey, so Mark traveled with Barnabas to Cyprus instead (Acts 15:38-39). Years later, however, Paul eventually reconciled with Mark and described him as *"very useful to me for ministry"* (2 Timothy 4:11).

Mark was also associated with both Paul and Peter in Rome.[6] In one letter, Peter referred to Mark as "*my son*" (1 Peter 5:13), meaning he was a spiritual mentor to Mark. Such evidence of their close relationship lends credibility to Papias' claim that Mark recorded Peter's testimony about Jesus. William L. Lane has also argued that Peter's sermon in Acts 2 closely parallels the content of the Gospel of Mark, which may reveal Peter's influence on this Gospel's composition.[7] In our own study, we'll see that Mark often reads like a disciple's firsthand account because of how it details Jesus' personal gestures and His audiences' reactions — so much that it can even be called the "Gospel of vividness."[8]

WHEN AND WHY

WAS THE GOSPEL OF MARK WRITTEN?

Have you ever experienced an emergency and needed immediate help from the police, fire department, or paramedics? Angst builds until the faint sounds of approaching sirens break through the air, and the first responders' arrival brings a fresh wave of hope.

The Gospel of Mark brought this kind of hope to humanity as the first written account of the good news of Jesus Christ to circulate through the ancient world.

Anecdotes of Jesus' life and teachings were first preserved in the memories of His disciples, which is hardly surprising given the extraordinary feats of ancient memory.[1] Memorization was especially valued and cultivated in Jewish culture. For instance, by age 10, Jewish boys usually memorized the entire Torah, or the first five books of the Old Testament.[2] Disciples in ancient Mediterranean society also carefully learned and committed their teachers' sayings to memory by taking notes, using repetition, and collaborating with other students.[3] The early Church would have passed along these accounts and teachings orally until Mark inscribed the first Gospel narrative.

DATE

Church tradition holds that Mark's Gospel was written just before or shortly after Peter's death in A.D. 64 or 65.[4] The majority of contemporary scholars still date Mark's Gospel writing around the mid-to-late 60s for at least three reasons:

1. This dating aligns with early Church tradition.

2. Mark's emphasis on following Jesus amid suffering fits the situation Christians faced in Rome during this time period.

3. Mark 13 seems to reflect the situation in Jerusalem before A.D. 70 (when the city was decimated by Rome).[5]

AUDIENCE

Although Mark did not identify his intended audience in the text, the most widely held understanding is that Mark wrote primarily to gentile Christians in Rome. Mark's Gospel explains some Jewish customs that would have been unfamiliar to gentiles, translates Aramaic and Hebrew phrases into Greek, uses a number of Latin words, and rarely quotes from the Old Testament. All of these text features are consistent with writing to a gentile audience.[6]

OCCASION

The Gospel of Mark was likely written during the reign of Nero, a Roman emperor who was overall despised and thought of as a madman even by his own people. The Roman aristocracy considered Nero a tyrant because he sidelined the senate, enforced high taxes, and leveled false accusations to confiscate wealth.[7]

On a summer night in A.D. 64, a great fire broke out in Nero's Rome and lasted six days and seven nights, destroying 10 of the city's 14 sections. In the devastating aftermath, rumors began to circulate that Nero himself had set fire to the city as inspiration to create an epic poem. Reports further claimed that he dressed as an actor, played his lyre, and sang as he watched the city burn from atop a tower.

Whether the fire was an accident or the result of Nero's deliberate actions is still uncertain. Either way, Nero could not squelch the rumors that he had set the city ablaze, so he pointed his finger at someone else: Christians.

Once the blame shifted to Christians, many were arrested and executed for their faith. And Nero didn't just kill Christians; he also used their deaths as entertainment. He dressed them in furs and fed them to dogs, crucified them, and turned them into human torches to light his gardens while he mingled with guests and rode around like a charioteer.[8] The Apostles Peter and Paul were among those killed during Neronian persecution. Eusebius' *Historia Ecclesiastica* records, "So it came about that this man [Nero], the first to be heralded as a conspicuous fighter against God, was led on to murder the apostles."[9]

PURPOSE

If Mark was written after the Great Fire of Rome, then we might consider it a pastoral response to the wave of persecution under Nero's rule. The first readers of Mark's good news were likely believers who faced horrible circumstances. Mark's task was to prepare an account of Jesus the Messiah in the context of suffering and martyrdom.[10]

So in his opening sentence, Mark 1:1 declared Jesus was the "*Son of God*" — and by implication, Nero was not. Even though Roman emperors often called themselves gods and claimed to have healing power, to inaugurate a new era, or to be "saviors" of their people, in the end, they were just ordinary men seated on temporary thrones.[11] Mark's Gospel clearly shows that Jesus is the only *true King* and *true Savior.*

Jesus' teaching in Mark 8:34 — *"take up [your] cross and follow me"* — also would have encouraged believers who sometimes literally bore crosses of persecution, reassuring them that their hardship was evidence of true commitment to Christ. And even to the ones who avoided cross-bearing discipleship by renouncing their faith, Mark's Gospel would have given hope of redemption. The narrative ends with an angelic messenger summoning the disciples even after they had abandoned and denied Jesus. In spite of our wounds and weaknesses, our Savior is always inviting His people to *"see him"* (Mark 16:7).

THE LANDSCAPE OF THE GOSPEL:

FIRST-CENTURY JUDEA AND SURROUNDING AREAS

We'll refer back to this map throughout our study of Mark, but for now, take a look at the geography of this map and see if you recognize any significant landmarks or locations. For instance, do you see the city where Jesus was from? The river where He was baptized? The city where the temple of God was located?

SIDON
TYRE
CAESAREA PHILIPPI
GALILEE
CAPERNAUM
BETHSAIDA
GENNASARET
DALMANUTHA
SEA OF GALILEE
NAZARETH
JORDAN RIVER
DECAPOLIS
SAMARIA
GERASENES
PEREA
JERICHO
BETHPHAGE
JERUSALEM
GETHSEMANE
BETHANY
JUDEA

WHAT ARE THE KEY THEMES

IN THE GOSPEL OF MARK?

CHRISTOLOGY (JESUS' IDENTITY AS THE CHRIST)

The Gospel of Mark establishes from the very beginning that Jesus is no ordinary human being. In the opening verse, Mark proclaims that "*Jesus Christ*" is the *"Son of God"* (Mark 1:1). Sometimes we may think of "Christ" as Jesus' last name, but it is actually a title for Jesus, translated from the Greek word *Christos*. It is parallel to the Hebrew word *Mashiach* (Messiah) in the Old Testament, meaning "Anointed One." Ancient Israelites anointed their kings by putting special oil on their heads, and Jesus came to reign as the ultimate Anointed One, whom God promised to raise up from King David's line (2 Samuel 7:12-16).

Mark 1:11 records that God's own voice also confirmed Jesus as His Son. Everything we will see Jesus do in the 16 chapters of Mark's Gospel — including casting out demons, healing the sick, calming a storm, walking on water, and raising the dead — displays His remarkable power and substantiates this initial proclamation.

The first half of Mark's narrative reaches its climax with Peter's words to Jesus: *"You are the Christ"* (Mark 8:29). The second half reaches its climax with a confession from the Roman centurion in charge of Jesus' crucifixion: *"Truly this man was the Son of God!"* (Mark 15:39). So by the book's conclusion, a spokesperson for Israel (Peter) and a spokesperson for the gentiles (the centurion) have both confessed who Jesus truly is.[1]

GOD'S UPSIDE-DOWN KINGDOM

How could Jesus be the Christ if He experienced the shame of a Roman crucifixion? This was an important question on the minds of Mark's first-century readers. One commentator notes, "From the Jewish standpoint, a crucified Messiah was an oxymoron, like calling a prisoner on death row, 'Mr. President.'"[2] Yet the Gospel of Mark carefully shows that Jesus' suffering and death was God's plan all along.

Despite their proximity to Jesus, even His own disciples repeatedly misunderstood this. Each time Jesus foretold His death, for instance, the disciples responded with ideas of earthly power and grandeur, once even asking for seats of honor beside the Messiah's throne. But God's Kingdom is not like earthly kingdoms built on pride and self-interest. King Jesus *"came not to be served but to serve, and to give his life as a ransom for many"* (Mark 10:45).

Jesus defied human expectations. He did not come to earth as a warrior king who would conquer Roman oppressors but as the suffering Servant who would lay down His life to achieve victory over Satan, sin, and death. The cross may have *appeared* a humiliating end for Jesus, but it actually served as the divinely appointed means of inaugurating the Kingdom of God.

DISCIPLESHIP

Jesus had many followers, but He specifically called 12 disciples who received private instruction from Him and special power to preach, heal, and cast out demons. These 12 left everything behind to follow Jesus, but they were not always "model disciples." Throughout Mark's Gospel, we'll see the 12 failed to understand Jesus' parables, were slow to learn, missed the significance of Jesus' miracles and teachings, lacked faith during hardships, and did not understand Jesus' role as Messiah.

Judas betrayed Jesus (Mark 14:45-46). Jesus' three closest disciples fell asleep when He asked them to pray (Mark 14:37-38). All the disciples abandoned Jesus when He was arrested (Mark 14:50). Peter denied knowing Jesus three times (Mark 14:72). Nonetheless, Jesus graciously chose, called, taught, forgave, empowered, and commissioned these imperfect people. He instructed them to take up their crosses and follow Him, to put themselves last and embrace lives of self-sacrifice for His Kingdom.

Mark's narrative does also include some positive examples of faith and discipleship: In Mark 5, we'll meet a woman who reached out to Jesus for healing and a man named Jairus who trusted that Jesus had power to resurrect the dead. A mother in Mark 7 had faith in Jesus' authority over demons; a father in Mark 9 chose to trust Jesus despite his own doubts; and a blind man in Mark 10 persisted in faith, received healing, and followed Jesus.

Still, there is only one *perfect model* for discipleship: the suffering, serving, and self-sacrificial Jesus Himself. And He calls us to follow His path.

MAJOR MOMENTS

WEEK 1

DAY 01 | MARK 1:1-8 — John the Baptist prepared the way for Jesus by calling people to repent and be baptized.

DAY 02 | MARK 1:9-20 — Jesus was baptized, then tempted in the wilderness, and He began calling His first disciples.

DAY 03 | MARK 1:21-45 — Jesus taught with authority, cast out demons, and healed a man with leprosy.

DAY 04 | MARK 2:1-12 — Jesus healed a paralyzed man and forgave his sins, revealing His divine authority.

DAY 05 | MARK 2:13-28 — Jesus called Levi, ate with sinners, and taught about fasting and the old covenant.

WEEK 2

DAY 06 | MARK 3:1-19 — Jesus healed on the Sabbath, faced growing opposition, and appointed the 12 apostles.

DAY 07 | MARK 3:20-35 — Jesus' family questioned Him, and He taught about the unforgivable sin and true kinship.

DAY 08 | MARK 4:1-20 — Jesus taught the parable of the sower and explained why He used parables.

DAY 09 | MARK 4:21-41 — Jesus taught more parables and calmed a storm, showing His power over nature.

DAY 10 | MARK 5:1-20 — Jesus delivered a man possessed by many demons, who then proclaimed Jesus' power.

WEEK 3

DAY 11 | MARK 5:21-43 — Jesus healed a woman and raised Jairus' daughter from the dead.

DAY 12 | MARK 6:1-13 — Jesus was rejected in His hometown and sent out the 12 to preach and heal.

DAY 13 | MARK 6:14-29 — Herod reluctantly executed John the Baptist after being manipulated by Herodias.

DAY 14 | MARK 6:30-56 — Jesus fed 5,000 people, walked on water, and healed the sick.

DAY 15 | MARK 7:1-23 — Jesus confronted the Pharisees about their traditions and taught that defilement comes from within.

WEEK 4

DAY 16 | MARK 7:24-37 — Jesus healed a deaf man and a gentile girl, showing that His mercy extends beyond Israel.

DAY 17 | MARK 8:1-21 — Jesus fed 4,000 people and warned His disciples about spiritual blindness and unbelief.

DAY 18 | MARK 8:22-38 — Jesus healed a blind man, predicted His own death, and called His followers to self-denial.

DAY 19 | MARK 9:1-13 — Jesus was transfigured before three disciples, confirming His identity as God's Son.

DAY 20 | MARK 9:14-29 — Jesus healed a boy with an unclean spirit the disciples could not cast out.

WEEK 5

DAY 21 | MARK 9:30-50 — Jesus predicted His death again and taught about humility and temptation.

DAY 22 | MARK 10:1-16 — Jesus taught about marriage and divorce, and He welcomed little children.

DAY 23 | MARK 10:17-34 — Jesus challenged a rich young man, then foretold His own death and resurrection again.

DAY 24 | MARK 10:35-52 — Jesus corrected His disciples' selfish ambition and healed Bartimaeus.

DAY 25 | MARK 11 — Jesus entered Jerusalem, cleansed the temple, and confronted religious leaders.

WEEK 6

DAY 26 | MARK 12:1-27 — Jesus told the parable of the tenants and answered difficult questions.

DAY 27 | MARK 12:28-44 — Jesus taught more, affirmed the greatest commandment, and praised a widow's offering.

DAY 28 | MARK 13:1-13 — Jesus predicted the destruction of the temple and warned of coming persecution.

DAY 29 | MARK 13:14-37 — Jesus foretold of tribulation before His return and urged watchfulness.

DAY 30 | MARK 14:1-31 — Jesus was anointed, predicted that He would be betrayed, and shared the Last Supper.

WEEK 7

DAY 31 | MARK 14:32-52 — Jesus prayed in Gethsemane and was arrested by a crowd led by Judas.

DAY 32 | MARK 14:53-72 — Jesus was tried before the Jewish council while Peter denied Him three times.

DAY 33 | MARK 15:1-32 — Jesus was condemned by Pilate, mocked, and crucified alongside criminals.

DAY 34 | MARK 15:33-47 — Jesus died, the temple curtain tore, and He was buried in a tomb.

DAY 35 | MARK 16 — Jesus rose from the dead and commissioned His disciples to proclaim the gospel.

WEEK ONE

DAY 1

MARK 1:1-8

John the Baptist prepared the way for Jesus by calling people to repent and be baptized.

When was the last time you had to introduce yourself to a group of new people? You might remember it as awkward or stressful as you shuffled through your thoughts and battled a rush of nerves. But in the end, you hopefully shared your name and something about yourself that would provide a framework for listeners to understand who you are.

The book of Mark begins with an introduction of "*Jesus Christ*" and gives us a framework for understanding who He is: "*the Son of God*" (Mark 1:1). This small phrase has huge implications. Jesus is unlike anyone else who has ever lived because He is a perfect human who is also fully divine.

While the other three Gospels begin with Jesus' birth (Luke), His human ancestry (Matthew), and His divine existence since the beginning of time (John), Mark's Gospel jumps right into Jesus' baptism narrative, which affirms His identity as declared in verse 1. To set the stage, Mark 1:2-4 also references prophetic scriptures from Isaiah 40:3 and Malachi 3:1 to describe the person who would baptize Jesus: John the Baptist.

> According to Mark 1:2-4, what was John the Baptist's purpose? (Note that John the Baptist is not to be confused with the Apostle and Gospel writer John.)

John the Baptist called the people of Judea and Jerusalem to repent and be baptized in the Jordan River. At first glance, we might not think this extraordinary because baptism is familiar to us in the modern Church. But to first-century Jews, this particular kind of baptism was anything but ordinary. They did not practice baptism like Christians do today; they practiced ceremonial washing according to Old Testament law, which was a method of ritual purification for specific situations and may not have included immersion.[1]

What was the reason for each of the following ceremonial washings prescribed by the law?

- Exodus 30:17-21: ______
- Numbers 19:11-12: ______
- Leviticus 15:10-11: ______
- Leviticus 11:24-25: ______

In these Old Testament passages, God required Jews to perform bodily cleansings for outward, ritual purity. But God led John to baptize in a way that called for *inner purification*, confession of sins, and preparation for the Lord's coming.

John's baptisms would have been more similar to the water-immersions that non-Jews had to go through when converting to Judaism. Native Jews thought they didn't need to be washed in this way because they were born into Jewish families and followed God's laws. In fact, Jews likely would have taken offense when John said they had to repent and be baptized like gentiles were as part of their conversion experience. Nevertheless, John called everyone, *"all the country of Judea and all Jerusalem"* (Mark 1:5), to come to God on the *same* terms.[2]

Why do you think this was important to prepare people for Jesus' ministry? How does Jesus also teach us that we *all* need the *same cleansing* to be right with God?

Mark's introduction of John the Baptist also includes a description of his seemingly strange food and clothing choices. Mark 1:6 says John ate locusts and honey, and he wore coarse camel hair and a leather belt. The Old Testament prophet Elijah had dressed this way in the past (2 Kings 1:8), so Jewish crowds may have considered John to be a reappearing of Elijah.[3] John's diet and clothing were also expressions of his willingness to sacrifice his own comfort and dignity for the sake of glorifying God.

In what ways do you sacrifice comfort and dignity for the sake of obeying and glorifying God? How does John's example challenge or encourage you?

In Mark 1:7-8, how did John compare himself to the One to come? What was the difference between John's baptism and the baptism to come?

John was waiting for the One who would *"baptize [people] with the Holy Spirit"* (Mark 1:8), as God's prophets had foretold. John would have been familiar with verses like Isaiah 32:15, which describes *"the Spirit [who] is poured upon us from on high."* John was waiting for this mighty One, whose sandal straps he wasn't even worthy to bend down and untie.

John was waiting for Jesus. And as he waited, he obeyed God day by day. May we do the same.

MORE ON "THE BAPTIST"

The title "John the Baptist" (or "John the Baptizer," as we see in some translations like the RSV Bible) comes from the Greek ho baptistes *or* ho baptizon, *meaning "one who baptizes." This refers to John's ministry of baptizing people in the Jordan River but is not connected to the Protestant "Baptist" denomination, which arose over 1,500 years later in the 17th century. Interestingly, the New Testament uses versions of both* baptistes *(Matthew 3:1; Matthew 11:11; Luke 7:20) and* baptizon *(Mark 1:4; Mark 6:14; Mark 6:24). Both simply describe John's role of baptizing people in water as part of his call to repentance.*

DAY 2

MARK 1:9-20

Jesus was baptized, then tempted in the wilderness, and He began calling His first disciples.

There's a lot we don't know about Jesus' early life. What was He like as a teenager? How did He relate to His earthly brothers and sisters? It's interesting to imagine ... but Mark's Gospel is efficient and emphatic in its focus on Jesus' last several years on earth, so the text zooms in on Jesus' ministry starting at the age of 30. At that point, Jesus was on the threshold of two events that would launch His public ministry: His baptism and His temptation in the wilderness.

First, let's look at Jesus' baptism. As we learned yesterday, Jesus was baptized by John, who was *"proclaiming a baptism of repentance for the forgiveness of sins"* (Mark 1:4) — yet Jesus was sinless. He had no transgressions to confess.

> So what was the purpose for Jesus' baptism? Look at the following scriptures for reference: Matthew 3:13-15, Luke 7:29-30, and Romans 6:3-4.

During Jesus' baptism, He saw *"the heavens being torn open"* in Mark 1:10! Something supernatural was happening. Elsewhere in Scripture, God had previously opened the heavens to signify divine revelation and show the nearness of His Kingdom (Ezekiel 1:1).[1] This event at Jesus' baptism is also often interpreted as a fulfillment of Isaiah 64:1, where the prophet prayed for God to "*rend the heavens and come down*."

The word "*torn*" in Mark 1:10 indicates that God was making Himself accessible to people in a new way. In fact, this is like a preview of what would happen after Jesus' resurrection in Mark 15:38: *"The curtain of the temple was torn in two,"* giving worshippers access to God like never before.[2]

> As the heavens opened at His baptism, Jesus saw God's Spirit descending like a dove and heard a voice from heaven. What did God the Father say in Mark 1:11? Why is this important?

After Jesus' baptism, Mark 1:12-13 says God's Spirit sent Him into the wilderness for 40 days, where He was tempted by Satan. We may be surprised to see God lead His Son in this way, but it's important to recognize that the God who led Jesus *to the desert* was with Him *through it* — and Jesus emerged victorious on the other side.

As modern readers, we can also bear in mind that the English word "*tempted*" in Mark 1:13 carries connotations in our culture that are not necessarily present in the scripture itself. We may see "*tempted*" as implying immorality or a desire to sin, as though Jesus wavered between sin and righteousness. But Jesus is not just a man, He's also *fully and perfectly God.* Jesus has *"no sin"* and *"appeared in order to take away sins"* as only God can do (1 John 3.5).

The Greek word *peirazo,* or "*tempted*" in the ESV translation of Mark 1:13, can also mean "tested." How might this shape your understanding of Jesus' wilderness experience?

Spiritual warfare was real for Jesus in His humanity, and it's real for us — though in a different way because we are sinners. It's challenging for us to remain faithful through the wilderness. How can Jesus' example encourage or equip us? (You may also want to read Ephesians 6:12-13 as you answer.)

When Jesus' physical body was weak, tired, and hungry from fasting (Matthew 4:2), Satan tested him, but Jesus proved faithful. Jesus left the wilderness as perfect as when He entered. Then He proclaimed good news in Galilee, announcing that *"the time is fulfilled, and the kingdom of God is at hand"* (Mark 1:15). In other words, it was time for Jesus to do what He came to earth to do.

So Jesus called four fishermen to be His first disciples — Simon Peter, Andrew, James, and John — and told them He would make them "*fishers of men*" (Mark 1:17).

What did these four disciples leave behind in Mark 1:18-20? What does this tell us about following Jesus?

After Jesus' baptism, what happened to John the Baptist in Mark 1:14? What does this tell us about following Jesus?

Jesus was doing a new thing, ushering in a new Kingdom, through His life and salvific work. His followers would face challenges, and we still do today ... yet no wildernesses, temptations, tangled nets, or even prisons of this world can keep us from His Kingdom. Our Savior promises He will make all things new (Revelation 21:5).

DAY 3

MARK 1:21-45

Jesus taught with authority, cast out demons, and healed a man with leprosy.

Some kids will ask for the same bedtime stories a hundred times and still enjoy "predicting" the ending. But as adults, we often find repetition boring. We want something fresh, new, and powerful.

In today's reading, the power of God was on full display when Jesus stepped into a synagogue, a Jewish assembly hall for religious teaching, in Capernaum. Capernaum was a fishing village on the northern shore of Israel's Sea of Galilee (which you can locate on the map on Page 13).

Instead of speaking like typical Jewish teachers, scribes, or scholars who appealed to the authority of other wise men — "as Moses said" or "as Rabbi So-and-So said" — Jesus taught in a new way that astonished the crowd.[1]

According to Mark 1:22, Jesus taught as "*one who had*" what?

The crowd detected that Jesus didn't just speak *about God*. Jesus spoke *as God*. And His words were coupled with mighty deeds that confirmed His dominion over both the physical and spiritual realm.[2] The first miracle recorded in Mark took place in this synagogue when there was a sudden outburst from *"a man with an unclean spirit"* (Mark 1:23). Here and throughout Mark's Gospel, this phrase describes someone experiencing demonic oppression or possession.

Does it surprise you that there was an unclean spirit in a house of scriptural study and prayer? Why or why not? How might Mark 1:23-24 help Christians understand the tactics of Satan or dark spiritual forces today?

In verse 24, what did the unclean spirit know about Jesus that the crowd did not know?

In Jesus' day, priests or self-proclaimed healers sometimes attempted exorcisms through incantations, magical formulas, or invoking the name of a higher spirit to expel the lower one. Exorcists would sometimes try to "scare out" a demon or even put a smelly root up the oppressed person's nose to try to revolt the unclean spirit.[3]

In Mark 1:25-27, how did Jesus deal with the unclean spirit? Why did this amaze the crowd?

By the 27th verse of Mark's Gospel, Jesus has both resisted Satan in the wilderness and cast out an unclean spirit, proving from the outset that demonic authority is no match for the Kingdom of God.

After leaving the synagogue, Jesus also demonstrated His authority over sickness and disease when he healed Simon Peter's mother-in-law. Word spread quickly, and by evening, people were bringing *"all who were sick or oppressed by demons"* to Jesus; *"the whole city was gathered"* to watch Him miraculously heal and restore (vv. 31-34).

Mark 1 concludes with Jesus' healing of a man with leprosy, a contagious skin disease that often resulted in slow and painful death. Lepers were also considered ceremonially unclean and were separated from family, friends, community, and religious life, further making leprosy one of the most dreaded diseases in the ancient world. Anyone who even *touched* a leper was also unclean until a priest declared him otherwise (Leviticus 14).[4]

Yet in Mark 1:40-41, when the leprous man begged for healing, what did Jesus do? Does this surprise you? Why or why not?

Touching the leprous man didn't make Jesus unclean. Instead, the opposite happened: *Jesus made the man clean*, demonstrating not only His power to heal but also to purify.

Interestingly, Jesus told the man to *"say nothing to anyone"* about his healing in verse 44. Scholars have termed this the "messianic secret," which we'll see throughout Mark's Gospel. Earlier, Jesus also silenced the demons who knew Him (vv. 24-25, 34).

Why might Jesus have wanted to keep His identity and miraculous work a secret at this point early in His ministry?

Did the man keep the secret in Mark 1:45? When have you experienced a miracle from God so amazing you just *had* to tell people about it? (Read Ephesians 2:8-9 for a reminder of the greatest miracle God has done in the life of every believer!)

DAY 4

MARK 2:1-12

Jesus healed a paralyzed man and forgave his sins, revealing His divine authority.

Have you ever had friends who supported you with their strength and faith when you couldn't carry yourself? Maybe they picked up the phone at 3 a.m. to talk you through a sleepless night. Maybe they brought meals to your house when a crisis left no room for you to think about dinner. Maybe they prayed when you had no words.

The paralyzed man in today's reading had friends like this, and we can all pray for the same in our lives. They were willing to carry his bed, climb up onto a rooftop, cut a man-sized hole in the ceiling, and carefully lower him down into the presence of Jesus.

According to Mark 2:2-4, why didn't the four men bring the paralyzed man through the front door? What does this tell us about Jesus' reputation at this point?

It matters who surrounds us. When Jesus saw the friends' faith, he healed the paralyzed man's greatest need — his spiritual need — saying, "*Son, your sins are forgiven*" (v. 5).

Read Mark 2:6-7. Who else was listening, and what was their reaction to Jesus' words?

The Old Testament taught that offering sacrifices in the temple was the only way for humans to atone for their sins. And the paralyzed man had neither made a temple sacrifice nor (as far as we know) expressed repentance. Furthermore, the Old Testament teaches that *only God* can forgive sins (Psalm 130:4; Jeremiah 33:8).[1] So to the Jewish scribes in Mark 2, Jesus' pronouncement of forgiveness was an outrageous affront to God's power and majesty, and they considered it blasphemy, or offensive and false speech against God.[2]

They failed to recognize that Jesus was not a normal Jewish rabbi. He had already demonstrated power over evil spirits and sickness and pronounced a leper "*clean*" in Mark 1, and here in this Capernaum home, He pronounced a sinner "*forgiven*" (Mark 2:5).

It's also important to note that when Jesus declared, *"Your sins are forgiven"* (v. 5), He used the passive voice, which listeners might have interpreted to mean that Jesus spoke on God's behalf, declaring forgiveness that God the Father had granted.[3] But Jesus clarified in verse 10 that *"the Son of Man has authority on earth to forgive sins."* In other words, Jesus was not just announcing forgiveness; He was *doing the forgiving*.

Since no one can forgive sins but God, what does verse 10 confirm (once again) about Jesus?

Apart from Jesus' words, the crowd had no evidence of the man's spiritual healing. So what did Jesus do next in verses 11-12?

Mark 1:1 calls Jesus the *"Son of God."* In Mark 2:10, Jesus called Himself the *"Son of Man,"* a title He used to refer to Himself more than any other — and one that carries significant meaning.

The prophet Daniel wrote of a Messianic King who is called the Son of Man. Take a moment to read Daniel 7:13-14, and fill in the chart below:

DANIEL 7:13-14 PROPHECIES	WHAT DOES THIS REVEAL ABOUT JESUS?	ADDITIONAL READING
"One like a son of man"		Philippians 2:7; Colossians 2:9
"With the clouds of heaven [He] came"		Matthew 24:30; Acts 1:9-11

DANIEL 7:13-14 PROPHECIES	WHAT DOES THIS REVEAL ABOUT JESUS?	ADDITIONAL READING
"He came to the Ancient of Days"		John 17:5
"To him was given dominion and glory and a kingdom"		Matthew 28:18; Revelation 11:15
"All peoples, nations, and languages should serve him"		Revelation 7:9-11
"His dominion is an everlasting dominion, which shall not pass away"		Luke 1:30-33

The title "Son of Man" alludes to how Jesus became a human being like us, descended from Adam, yet He is also the divine Ruler prophesied in Daniel 7 who reigns forever. He has all power both to heal and to forgive. *"Which is easier"* is an ironic question in Mark 2:9 — because nothing is difficult for Jesus.

And His eternal reign is central to our hope. Our temporary, fragile bodies are subject to brokenness on earth, but believers eagerly await the day when our Lord will transform our bodies *"to be like his glorious body"* (Philippians 3:20-21). Jesus gives us eternal life, and we don't have to climb on a roof to be near Him. He holds us even now, and *"no one will snatch [us] out of [His] hand"* (John 10:28).

DAY 5

MARK 2:13-28

Jesus called Levi, ate with sinners, and taught about fasting and the old covenant.

If you're living in the 21st century, chances are, you're paying taxes. And no matter how honorable the government, it never feels great to give away your hard-earned money.

Imagine how it must have felt for the Jews to pay imperial taxes to the Roman government, whose presence many despised, in addition to paying regional and local taxes to Roman-appointed rulers. To make matters worse, tax officials were often dishonest, charging higher fees than Rome required and lining their own pockets with the excess.[1] Herod Antipas was the tetrarch (a local ruler under Roman oversight) of Galilee and Perea, and the tax collectors who worked for him were particularly unpopular, considered the vilest of men.

When a Jew became a tax collector, he became an outcast and a disgrace to his family, was disqualified as a witness in Jewish courts, and was excommunicated from the synagogue.[2] If a tax collector entered a Jew's house, everything in the house was considered ceremonially unclean.[3]

But we know already from this week's Bible study that Jesus does not distance Himself from the unclean. He leans in and offers to reverse their condition.

> What did Jesus do in Mark 2:14 when He met the tax collector Levi in Capernaum? (Note that this was a coastal town in Herod Antipas' territory, and Levi was likely collecting a toll on fish or other goods in transit from neighboring territories.)[4]

> Jesus' encounter with Levi is also recorded in other Gospel accounts. What else do we learn about him in Matthew 9:9 and Luke 5:27-28?

Most scholars believe this tax collector was called by two names: Levi and Matthew. However, some suggest Mark may have called him "Levi" because he was a Levite, a member of Israel's priestly tribe (Deuteronomy 18:5). If this was the case, Levi would have been especially hated by the Jewish community for choosing the despised occupation of tax collecting over his religious calling.[5]

But to this very man with whom no other rabbi or religious leader would have dared to associate, Jesus said, *"Follow me"* (Mark 2:14). And Levi did! He was reviled by society, but he was loved by God.

Luke 5:29 says Levi celebrated his commitment to Jesus by throwing a *"great feast."* Who else was at this dinner party in Levi's home, per Mark 2:15? Why were they there?

The Pharisees were influential religious figures who believed they were the best interpreters of God's Word. They pledged to obey all aspects of both God's law and what they saw as pious human traditions, holding strict standards for ceremonial purity.[6]

It comes as no surprise that members of this self-righteous group would have questioned Jesus' decision to eat with tax collectors and sinners. Pharisees would *never* fraternize with such riffraff! Interestingly, the Greek term for "*sinners*" in Mark 2:16 (*hamartolos*) could refer to people who were actually disobeying God or simply to common people who did not live by the Pharisaic standards for righteousness.[7]

In Mark 2:17, how did Jesus respond to the Pharisees' question? What did this reveal about their spiritual wellness (or lack thereof)?

"*John's disciples*" in verse 18 were followers of John the Baptist, and they fasted alongside the Pharisees in the tradition of the Old Testament: as a sign of deep sorrow, repentance, and longing for God. But Jesus' disciples were enjoying a feast. They would even pluck grain on the Sabbath too (vv. 23-28).

According to Mark 2:19-20, why were Jesus' disciples not fasting? What does this teach us about being disciples of Jesus today?

In verse 22, Jesus spoke a parable about wineskins to confront the Pharisees' legalism and illustrate the significance of His ministry. His metaphor pulled from imagery that was familiar to His first-century audience, so let's make sure we also understand it as modern readers:

Wine in the ancient world was stored in animal skins sewn together, and when new wine fermented inside this container, the wineskin would stretch. But if new wine was poured into an already-stretched wineskin, it would burst.

Jesus' message was this: The Kingdom of God could not be "poured into" the current (already-stretched) institutions of Judaism. The old covenant would soon give way to the new because Jesus had come to inaugurate a new era of salvation.[8]

WEEK 1

WEEKEND REFLECTION

& PRAYER

THE COST OF DISCIPLESHIP

In the first two chapters of Mark, Jesus called His first five disciples. When Jesus said *"follow me"* to a group of fishermen in Mark 1:17, Simon Peter, Andrew, James, and John turned from their nets and followed Him. It may not seem like much to leave behind, but these nets supported their livelihood (and they were seemingly making good money, given the reference to hired servants in Mark 1:20). Leaving their nets meant leaving behind financial security. And Levi (Matthew) did the same in Mark 2:14 when he left behind his lucrative position as a tax collector to follow Jesus.

Not only did these disciples leave their jobs, but they left their families. The reference to Peter's mother-in-law in Mark 1:30 indicates he had a wife who remained in Galilee while he followed Jesus. In Mark 1:20, we read that James and John left their father, Zebedee. Later, Peter said to Jesus, *"See, we have left everything and followed you"* (Mark 10:28).

The disciples chose Jesus over everything because Jesus is *worth more than anything* the world has to offer.

So how does the cost of discipleship translate to us today? Are we to leave behind our jobs and families?

Not necessarily. But pursuing Jesus does require sacrifice, whether these or others. As the late missionary Jim Elliot once wrote, "He is no fool who gives what he cannot keep to gain that which he cannot lose."[1]

Sacrificial discipleship means loving our enemies instead of seeking revenge, giving even when it's hard, and sacrificing time to study the Bible and pray. It could mean crossing international borders to share the gospel in a remote village, or it could mean stepping outside of our comfort zone to share our testimony with a co-worker or invite a neighbor to church.

Wherever Jesus leads, may our hearts be willing to follow.

PRAYER

Heavenly Father, please help me to deny myself, give me courage to step outside of what's comfortable and familiar, and embolden me to share the good news of Your Kingdom. Mold me and shape me into a faithful disciple. I want to live like Jesus and go where Your Spirit leads me. In Jesus' name, amen.

NOTES

NOTES

WEEK TWO

DAY 6

MARK 3:1-19

Jesus healed on the Sabbath, faced growing opposition, and appointed the 12 apostles.

In a world of constant hustle, it's difficult to slow down even when we desperately need rest. Modern life moves at what feels like a breakneck pace — but still, rest isn't a new human need, and restlessness isn't a new problem.

When God gave the Ten Commandments long ago, He commanded His people to do no work on the Sabbath, a complete day of rest once per week. It was meant to be a day to worship God and remember that He was their Creator, Deliverer, and Provider (Exodus 20:8-11; Deuteronomy 5:15). The Jewish people observed the Sabbath from sundown on Friday to sundown on Saturday.

What was the punishment for breaking the Sabbath, according to Exodus 31:14?

Leviticus 20:3-4 describes the punishment for practicing child sacrifice. How does this compare to the Sabbath-breaking penalty? What does this tell us about how serious the Sabbath day was to God and His people?

By the time Jesus lived on earth, Jewish scribes and Pharisees had formulated 39 classes of actions prohibited as "work" on the Sabbath day. Each of the 39 classes was further detailed until there were several hundred prohibited actions (e.g., making a knot, extinguishing a fire, writing two letters).[1] Violations typically resulted in fines or public beatings while capital punishment was reserved for those who willfully rejected the Sabbath.[2]

In today's reading, Pharisees *"watched Jesus, to see whether he would heal him on the Sabbath, so that they might accuse him"* of breaking their rules (Mark 3:2). But as we already saw in Mark 2:27-28, Jesus taught that God gave the law of the Sabbath for human *benefit*, so human needs took precedence over Pharisaical policies.[3] This created tension when Jesus healed a man in the synagogue *"with a withered hand"* — on the day of rest (Mark 3:1).

Some Pharisees allowed for medical treatment on the Sabbath if the medicine was prepared earlier in the week. Others only permitted treatment if a person's life was in danger. They even argued among themselves whether prayer for the sick was permissible on the Sabbath![4]

Knowing this, what question did Jesus ask the Pharisees in Mark 3:4? How did they respond?

Jesus said whether He chose to heal the man or not, either decision would have meant doing "work" on the Sabbath. As much as curing the man was a good work, refusing to cure him would have been an evil work.[5]

When Jesus restored the man's hand, how did the Pharisees react in Mark 3:6? In what ways did they prioritize their work-related rules and traditions over people?

Jesus chose compassion over strict compliance to man-made rules. What's one situation in your life where you can follow His example?

Of all things, Jesus' act of *healing a man* was the breaking point for the Pharisees. Along with the Herodians (political supporters of Herod Antipas), they began to plot against Jesus. But even as opposition grew, so did Jesus' popularity with the people. Large crowds followed Him in Mark 3:7-10, including many who suffered from diseases and desperately sought to touch the Healer.

Finally, Jesus went up on a mountainside away from the crowds and called 12 men whom He designated as His "*apostles*" (Mark 3:14), meaning "sent ones" or commissioned representatives.

According to Mark 3:14-15, what were these apostles called to do, and what authority would they have?

What do these verses further reveal about the source and purpose of Jesus' authority as compared to the Pharisees who thought of themselves as religious authorities?

WHAT IS THE DIFFERENCE BETWEEN A "DISCIPLE" AND AN "APOSTLE"?

Like "disciple," the term "apostle" existed before Jesus' time and was even used in secular contexts. It comes from the Greek apostolon, *and by itself, it simply means "sent one." Jesus was the first person to use the word "apostle" as a reference to an office within the Christian faith. In Scripture, this word is applied to Jesus' 12 original disciples and later to Matthias, Paul, Barnabas, and Jesus' brother James. We might think of these men as "capital A" Apostles: They were eyewitnesses to the resurrected Jesus and were personally commissioned by Him. (Paul's encounter with Jesus in Acts 9 qualified him to be an Apostle.) The miracles and signs that accompanied these Apostles' ministry also confirmed their special authority and validated their writing of Scripture.*

THE 12 APOSTLES OF JESUS

Mark 3 tells us about how, where, and why Jesus called His 12 apostles, and Luke 6:13-16 also identifies each of the 12 men by name. Here's a little more information about them:

JOHN

- Son of Zebedee
- James' brother
- One of Jesus' three closest disciples
- Known as the "disciple whom Jesus loved"
- Fisherman by trade
- Assumed author of the Gospel of John as well as 1 John, 2 John, 3 John, and Revelation
- Died of old age after A.D. 98

THADDAEUS

- Also called Judas or Jude
- Son of James
- Died as a martyr

JUDAS ISCARIOT

- Betrayed Jesus with a kiss
- Took his own life after Jesus' crucifixion

BARTHOLOMEW

- Closely associated with Philip
- Perhaps also known as Nathanael
- Died as a martyr

JAMES

- Also called James the Greater
- Son of Zebedee
- John's brother
- One of Jesus' three closest disciples
- Fisherman by trade
- King Herod Agrippa killed him by sword

THOMAS

- Nicknamed "Doubting Thomas"
- Martyred by spears in India

SIMON

- Also called Simon the Zealot
- Further details of life and death not certain

PETER

- Also called Simon Peter, Simeon, or Cephas
- One of Jesus' three closest disciples
- Fisherman by trade
- Crucified around A.D. 64 by Emperor Nero

JAMES

- Son of Alphaeus
- Further details of life and death not certain

MATTHEW

- Also called Levi
- Tax collector by trade
- Assumed author of the Gospel of Matthew
- Cause and date of death not certain

ANDREW

- Peter's brother
- Fisherman by trade
- Crucified around A.D. 60

PHILIP

- From Bethsaida
- Cause and date of death not certain

*While Matthias was also an apostle, he is usually not listed as one of the 12 disciples because he was appointed *by* the disciples, and he became an apostle after Judas Iscariot's death.

DAY 7

MARK 3:20-35

Jesus' family questioned Him, and He taught about the unforgivable sin and true kinship.

"It's not true! I didn't say that. That's not the whole story. Let me explain ..."

If you've ever been falsely accused, you may have used these kinds of words to defend yourself, feeling frustrated and powerless as you scrambled to prove your innocence or clear your name. In today's reading, Jewish religious leaders made false accusations against Jesus, and even His own family made an untrue statement about Him. But instead of launching into panicked self-defense, Jesus turned two troubling situations into teaching opportunities.

As Jesus' popularity grew among the people, crowds surrounded Him and His disciples to such an extent that *"they could not even eat"* (Mark 3:20). When Jesus' family heard about this in verse 21, how did they react, and what did they plan to do?

What does John 7:5 say about Jesus' brothers? Knowing this, are you surprised by their actions? Why or why not?

Jesus' urgent desire to minister — more than He desired to eat — led His family to call Him *"out of his mind"* in Mark 3:21, indicating misunderstanding and unbelief on their part.[1] It might come as a surprise that even Jesus' mother was traveling alongside these unbelieving brothers. Of all people, Mary knew Jesus was the *"Son of the Most High"* (Luke 1:32), and she recognized Jesus' power to perform miracles (John 2:1-11). So why did she go to the house with the brothers who were determined to interrupt Jesus' ministry?

Bible commentator William L. Lane answers: "It is unnecessary to suppose that Mary also suspected that Jesus had lost his grasp on reality. Her presence ... however, indicates her faith was insufficient to resist the determination of her sons to restrain Jesus and bring him home."[2] We do not know whether the family's motive was to protect Jesus from danger, to protect their own family reputation, or something else, but we do know they meant to silence Jesus and thus (even if unwittingly) opposed the will of God.[3]

Read Mark 3:33-35. What question did Jesus ask, and how did He then answer His own question?

Jesus redefined His family. He was not just thinking of blood relatives but of spiritual relatives, including all who embrace Him and the gospel message. To do the will of God is to be part of the family of God (Mark 3:35).

Sometimes God's people are even more like family to us than our biological or earthly families. How have you experienced this in your own life or seen it in the lives of fellow believers?

We might naturally expect Jesus' family members to be the *insiders* in His ministry, but a newly defined family of faith surrounded Him in the house in Mark 3:31-35. By the same token, we might expect religious leaders to be the *primary recipients* of God's favor, but Jesus poured out blessings of healing and forgiveness on outcasts and sinners who responded to Him with faith and repentance.[4]

Sadly, the scribes and Pharisees responded to Jesus with unbelief and hard-heartedness. One particular group of scribes traveled all the way from Jerusalem to Capernaum, nearly a hundred miles, a four-to-five-day journey on foot, just so they could confront Jesus in Mark 3:22-30. They made accusations far worse than His brothers'.

Let's look at these accusations and Jesus' response using the chart below:

SCRIBES' ACCUSATIONS IN MARK 3:22	JESUS' RESPONSE
"He is possessed by ________________ ..." (Note: This Hebrew word literally means "lord of dung" and is a name for Satan.)	According to Mark 3:29-30, what *"eternal sin"* were the scribes in danger of committing by uttering this accusation?
"... by the __________ of ______________, he casts out the demons."	According to Mark 3:23-26, what was the flaw in their logic?

The scribes considered Jesus' work unlawful and equated Him to a magician using demonic sorcery. But Jesus was not possessed by an unclean spirit — He possesses the Spirit of God![5] Jesus was casting out demons by the power of the Holy Spirit, so to attribute those exorcisms to Satan was to blaspheme *against the Holy Spirit Himself.* These leaders and experts in religious law were dangerously close to committing a sin that *"never has forgiveness"* (v. 29) — the sin of willfully and permanently rejecting the God who is our only source of eternal salvation.[6]

Jesus talked about *"bind[ing] the strong man,"* referring symbolically to Satan, in Mark 3:27. How has the Gospel of Mark so far shown us Jesus' unique strength to overpower the enemy? Where in your life today do you most need to experience this strength, and how does today's reading reassure you?

DAY 8

MARK 4:1-20

Jesus taught the parable of the sower and explained why He used parables.

Have you ever felt like you have more enemies than friends? In this week's reading, we've seen Jesus offer His friendship to many who rejected it. The Pharisees resolved to kill Him, the scribes accused Him of colluding with demonic spirits, and even His brothers said He was "*out of his mind*" (Mark 3:21). Yet while some responded to Jesus' ministry with hostility and confusion, others received His message with faith and gladness.

What causes people to respond so differently to Jesus? One answer is found in His parable of the sower in Mark 4:1-9. A parable is a saying or story that illustrates an important truth in terms of a familiar, real-life situation. The Greek word *parobole* means "juxtaposition, comparison, illustration."[1] Jewish rabbis did not typically speak in parables, but this was Jesus' preferred method of teaching. In fact, the first three Gospels record around 60 parables of Jesus![2]

According to Mark 4:10-12, why did Jesus choose to speak in parables?

Only those who listened astutely — and whose ears were opened by God Himself — would understand Jesus' parables and learn "*the secret of the kingdom of God*" (v. 11). Through Jesus' words and deeds, the gospel that was once mysterious was now being unveiled to His disciples.[3]

Matthew 13:34-35 records an additional reason Jesus used parables. What is it? Also read Psalm 78:2, and consider why it's important that Jesus' parables fulfilled ancient prophecy.

In Mark 4:3-8, Jesus began to tell a parable using the familiar image of a farmer who was sowing seeds, but not all the seeds fell on good, well-prepared soil. The conditions of the ground and the weather directly affected the seeds' productivity.[4]

As you read the rest of this parable in verses 3-8, complete the three shaded columns of the chart below:

SEED PLACEMENT	GROUND CONDITION	OUTCOME	SPIRITUAL MEANINGS
"Some seed fell along the path ..." (v. 4).	Hard-packed (ancient paths were often dirt trodden down by travelers).	The seed is exposed and eaten by hungry birds.	
"Other seed fell on rocky ground ..." (vv. 5-6).			
"Other seed fell among thorns ..." (v. 7).			
"Other seeds fell into good soil ..." (v. 8).			

When Jesus was alone with a group of disciples, including the 12, He explained that the seed in this parable represents God's Word. Just as seed falls on different soils, the Word of God falls on different hearers. Some never grasp the message of God's Truth, some are discouraged by difficulties, and others are seduced by prosperity; however, some remain committed to the gospel.[5]

Carefully read Mark 4:14-20, and then go back to the chart above. In the final, right-hand column, make some notes about the spiritual meanings of each soil, seed, and outcome. How does Jesus' parable deepen or change your understanding of why people respond differently to the gospel, even people you know personally?

Jesus illustrated several incorrect responses to Him, including *"fall[ing] away"* during "*persecution*" (Mark 4:17). This was important for Jesus' first listeners (Jews living under Roman oppression), and it remains important for us today. Persecution or opposition of various kinds will always be a reality for people who receive the gospel. But when the trials come, by God's grace, those with deep spiritual roots will persevere.[6]

Remember that Mark also likely wrote this Gospel during Neronian persecution of the early Church (see Page 11), so Jesus' parable of the sower also may have served as a strong warning to first-century Christians who were tempted to renounce their faith under the growing threat of danger and death.[7] At the same time, this parable would have profoundly encouraged believers who were staying faithful to Jesus: "*the ones who hear the word and accept it and bear fruit, thirtyfold and sixtyfold and a hundredfold*" (Mark 4:20).

As a Christ follower, what challenges make it difficult for you to stay grounded in God's Word? What helps you persevere and bear fruit?

DAY 9

MARK 4:21-41

Jesus taught more parables and calmed a storm, showing His power over nature.

In the parable of the sower that we read yesterday, Jesus taught about the nature of how human hearts respond to God's Word. In today's three parables, Jesus described God's Kingdom, or the nature of His reign. Let's explore each one.

We'll start with the parable of the lamp in Mark 4:21-23. **The key takeaway from this parable is that the Kingdom of God is fully revealed in Christ.**

So far in our study, we've read that Jesus silenced demons who recognized His divinity, commanded a healed man not to tell anyone about his healing, and spoke in parables so not all hearers would understand ... at least not yet. But in Mark 4:22, Jesus said, "*Nothing is hidden except to be made manifest.*" This refers to how, after Jesus' death and resurrection, the gospel would be fully revealed and His disciples would be commissioned to go out and share it with the world (Mark 16:15-18).

Jesus also described this truth using the image of a lamp. People at the time used small clay lamps that had to be set on a stand to illuminate a room. Putting a basket over a lamp would conceal the light and possibly even extinguish the flame.[1]

> What are some examples of ways Christians *reveal* the light of Christ like a lamp? What are some ways we might *conceal* the light, and how can we remove these "baskets"?

Next, in Mark 4:26-29, Jesus compared the Kingdom of God to a man scattering seeds. **The key takeaway from this parable is that the Kingdom of God will surely flourish.**

> In verses 27-28, what did the man do while the seed grew *"by itself"*? What might this reveal about divine power versus human power in God's Kingdom?

If the farmer in this parable represents Christ's followers, the message is this: When we share the gospel, we are but seed scatterers. The power of God brings the harvest. For first-century readers of Mark, this would have especially encouraged disciples who were experiencing rejection of their message or feeling frustration from not understanding God's plan.[2]

On the other hand, we could also interpret the farmer as a representation of Jesus: He sowed seeds with His preaching and ministry, and nothing could prevent the harvest of His faithful work.[3] In other words, no amount of opposition can thwart God's plan in Christ. His seeds *will* grow and yield.

Jesus also compared the Kingdom of God to a mustard seed in Mark 4:30-32, which was considered the smallest of all seeds in first-century Israel — but far from inconsequential. **The key takeaway from this parable is that the Kingdom of God will spread and accomplish great things.** The tiny mustard seed sometimes grows into a shrub more than 10 feet tall.[4] In the parable, it becomes such a large plant that birds make nests in its shade.

How does this compare to the trees prophesied in Ezekiel 17:23, Ezekiel 31:6, and Daniel 4:12-17? What do these verses and Jesus' parable suggest about how God's Kingdom offers refuge and spiritual shelter?

Interestingly, mustard is a weed — invasive and fast-growing. Therefore, this parable may also allude to the rapid spread of God's Kingdom.[5] When Jesus died and rose again, He would have only about 100 close followers, but God's Kingdom would quickly grow and expand across the Mediterranean and the world, transforming millions of lives and changing the course of history.[6]

Finally, not only did Jesus use imagery of nature in His Kingdom parables, but He demonstrated power and authority over nature itself in Mark 4:35-41.

What did Jesus do here that proved His divine authority over nature? How did His disciples react? (Note that there are multiple reactions, emotions, and questions here, so take a moment to really consider each one.)

What does Jesus' power over nature teach us about how we react to Him during our own "storms" of life?

DAY 10

MARK 5:1-20

Jesus delivered a man possessed by many demons, who then proclaimed Jesus' power.

"*Peace! Be still!*" These are the words Jesus spoke when He rebuked the wind and calmed the sea in Mark 4:39. Afterward, in today's reading, Jesus was confronted by a man who had a storm swirling inside of him — because he was possessed by an unclean spirit. And again Jesus spoke peace, this time not to the seas but to a soul.

In Mark 5:1, Jesus and His disciples sailed to the country of Gerasenes, which was part of the Decapolis, a group of 10 cities heavily influenced by Greek culture. (You can locate it on the map on Page 13.)

This was the first time in Jesus' ministry that He entered a gentile territory. Why might this be significant? (See Romans 1:16 and Matthew 12:21.)

Mark 5:2 says, *"Immediately there met [Jesus] out of the tombs a man with an unclean spirit."* We do not know this man's name, but from the text, we can learn several things about him:

1. *"HE LIVED AMONG THE TOMBS"* (MARK 5:3).

Not only was he ceremonially unclean because of the spirit dwelling within him, but he was also unclean because of his physical dwelling place — among (and likely within) caves where bodies were buried. Numbers 19:11 says a person was ceremonially defiled when they touched a corpse; therefore, tombs were unclean places.[1]

2. HE WAS TORMENTED BOTH EMOTIONALLY AND PHYSICALLY (MARK 5:4-5).

The unclean spirit(s) inhabiting the man kept him in emotional agony, constantly "*crying out*," and also made him physically self-destructive. He was strong — even chains and irons could not keep him bound — but this "strength" was to his own detriment.

3. THE SPIRIT WITHIN HIM RECOGNIZED JESUS (MARK 5:6-7).

Perhaps meaning to challenge Jesus, the spirit first drove the man to run toward Him, but then he collapsed in submission before the "*Son of the Most High God.*" The spirit that had relentlessly tormented this man now feared being tormented by Jesus, so the demon begged for mercy. But at Jesus' command, the spirit's fate was sealed.

4. THERE WERE ACTUALLY MANY UNCLEAN SPIRITS INSIDE THIS MAN (MARK 5:9).

Up until this verse, the text refers to "*an unclean spirit*" in the singular, meaning one spirit. But when Jesus asked the spirit its name, "*he replied, 'My name is Legion, for we are many.'*"

> Who else in the Bible was possessed by multiple spirits, according to Luke 8:2? What did Jesus do for her? How does this show that He (and all who believe in Him!) can never be "outnumbered" by the enemy?

A legion was a Roman military unit of approximately 6,000 soldiers. This doesn't necessarily mean the man in Mark 5 was possessed by 6,000 evil spirits, but there certainly were a lot.[2] When Jesus was expelling these many spirits, they begged Him to let them enter a herd of pigs (which were considered unclean animals). Although Jesus permitted this in Mark 5:13, the arrangement was short-lived.

> In verse 13, what happened to the pigs? How does this confirm Jesus' complete power to destroy darkness, not bending to any of its demands?

5. THE HEALED MAN WANTED TO FOLLOW JESUS (MARK 5:18).

No longer was his home among the dead. The healed man sought to leave Gerasenes and physically go with Jesus, the living One, but Jesus had other plans.

In Mark 5:19, what assignment did Jesus give the man? How is this different from His command to the man He healed from leprosy in Mark 1:44?

Why did Jesus silence one person and encourage the other to go and tell? The difference may have something to do with location. Jesus was careful to protect the "messianic secret" in Mark 1 while He was in Jewish territory, where people were likely to misunderstand His divine purpose. But in gentile territory, news of His power could spread without hindering His mission.

Praise God that the power and authority Jesus demonstrated in today's reading gives us clear confirmation: The Kingdom of God crushes the kingdom of Satan. A hymn by church reformer Martin Luther also echoes this truth: "[Satan's] rage we can endure, for lo, his doom is sure."

How does God's power over Satan comfort you today? How does it enable you to face the future without fear? (See also 1 John 4:4 and Romans 16:20.)

UNCLEAN SPIRITS
& DEMON POSSESSION

Throughout Mark's narrative, we see mention of "*unclean spirits*" and "*demons*," with Mark using both terms seemingly interchangeably. There is no physical description nor explanation of the origin of these dark beings. We only know they wreaked havoc on the people they inhabited (Mark 5:2-5; Mark 9:17-18), they often recognized Jesus as the Son of God (Mark 3:11), and they were no match for His power and authority (Mark 1:27).

In the Old Testament, things that were unclean prohibited a person from coming into the presence of God, so it made sense for Jews to call demons or evil spirits "unclean" because they had the same effect: oppressing or taking control of a human and separating them from the presence of God.[1]

The idea of these supernatural beings might bring discomfort to modern readers — it certainly lies outside the focus of most scientific inquiry. We might even be tempted to reduce demon possession to a medical condition, but this would be a mistake. Although there may sometimes be overlap between spiritual affliction and medical symptoms (like the description of what sounds like a seizure caused by a demon in Mark 9:17-18), Mark made a clear distinction between demonic possession and other types of sickness. When a person was sick, Mark wrote that Jesus "*healed*" them, but when a person was demon-possessed, he specifically wrote that Jesus "*cast out*" the spirits (e.g., Mark 1:34).[2]

How, then, should we respond to the reality of supernatural forces like these? Bible commentators like Mark L. Strauss encourage a balanced approach of neither obsessing over them nor denying their existence. As believers, we recognize that Satan's forces are real and active in the world, and we put on the armor of God to defend ourselves against attacks (Ephesians 6:10-20). We also remember and stand firm in the truth about our Savior and King: **Jesus Christ has already won the victory** (Colossians 2:15).[3]

WEEK 2

WEEKEND REFLECTION & PRAYER

POWER OVER ALL THINGS

The storm in Mark 4:35-41 must have been particularly violent to make Jesus' disciples — several of whom were experienced fishermen — tremble with fear. But why did they worry instead of trusting in the power and presence of Jesus, who was on the boat with them? The disciples feared the storm even though they had experienced Jesus' ministry, heard Him teach with authority, and seen Him heal the sick and cast out demons.

As Jews who knew Old Testament scriptures like Jonah 1:4-16 and Exodus 14:21-31, the 12 must have known that God wields power over the wind and sea — but they had never seen any *human* who had power to command the elements of nature.

Still, Jesus expected them to have faith based on all they had seen Him do. And as we ourselves witness His miraculous ministry through Mark's Gospel account, we might even hear Jesus' words in Mark 4:39-40 as His words to us: *"Peace! Be Still! ... Why are you so afraid? Have you still no faith?"*

We sometimes wrestle with doubt and fear as life's storms rage. Amid divorce, betrayal, grief, loss, medical diagnoses, financial hardships, and more, we might wonder if our crisis is too big and a miracle is too far-fetched. But there is no storm too big and no sea too violent for our Lord Jesus to calm. *We* are the ones who often put imagined limitations on His power. In reality, His power is unlimited.

PRAYER

Heavenly Father, You know the storms of life that I am facing now and the ones to come. Help me to have faith in Your power to calm every storm. Remind me also that You are a healer. You have the power to do all things — impossible things are possible for You! The winds and waves obey Your commands, and demons flee at the sound of Your voice. I trust You to speak peace in my life. In Jesus' name, amen.

NOTES

NOTES

WEEK THREE

DAY 11

MARK 5:21-43

Jesus healed a woman and raised Jairus' daughter from the dead.

When our account balance is dwindling, anxiety grows every time another bill arrives. When our marriage feels colder and colder, fear and insecurity seep in. When we give our best efforts only to keep coming up empty-handed, a season of waiting becomes a season of frustration. Sometimes the tensions of life build so slowly we don't even recognize them until a wave of desperation hits — knocking us flat.

In today's reading, Jesus met two individuals who were at critical points in their lives, teetering on the brink of despair and desperate for a miracle. Human solutions had failed them, and in their desperation, each went looking for Jesus.

Jesus was once again in Jewish territory starting in Mark 5:21, having traveled back across the Sea of Galilee after healing the demon-possessed man in Gerasenes. Now Jairus, a ruler of the Jewish synagogue, came to Jesus and fell at His feet.

> In verses 23-24, what did Jairus ask, and how did Jesus respond? How is this different from how we've seen other Jewish religious leaders approach Jesus in Mark's Gospel?

Before Jesus could get to Jairus' sick daughter, the story shifts to another seeker: a woman in the crowd who was desperate for His healing touch. The text tells us she had *"a discharge of blood for twelve years"* (v. 25). While we can only assume the details of her condition, many scholars interpret her sickness as some form of uterine bleeding.

This would have made it impossible to bear children, which carried immense stigma in the Ancient Near East. For this reason, depending on her age when the condition began, she was likely either unmarried or divorced. She also would have struggled financially since women could not easily earn much income on their own, and we know from verse 26 that she *"spent all that she had"* on remedies.[1] She was hurting physically, socially, financially ... and worse still, spiritually. According to Old Testament law, her incessant bleeding would have rendered her ceremonially unclean as well.

Read Leviticus 15:25-28. What other things became unclean if touched by a woman with this affliction? How do you think this affected her relationships with people and with God?

This woman wouldn't have been allowed into the inner courts of the temple (see the "Map of the Temple in Jesus' Day" on Page 129). For 12 years, she would have been prohibited from entering the place of worship and participating in religious ceremonies. Why? Because nothing unclean can enter into the perfect presence of the Lord.

Yet now this woman stepped through the crowd into the presence of Jesus — and *touched Him!*

What happened when the woman touched Jesus' garments in Mark 5:28-34? How did Jesus react?

In ancient times, many believed a healer's power could be accessed through clothing they had touched or worn (an idea reflected later in Mark 6:56 and Acts 19:11-12), so it's not surprising the woman reached for Jesus' garments.[2] But it actually was not Jesus' clothing that healed the woman. When Jesus spoke to her, He explained that she was healed by her *"faith"* (Mark 5:34).

Similarly, Jesus also called Jairus to have faith in verse 36. As Jesus was speaking to the now healed woman, someone announced that Jairus' daughter had died. Jesus was too late ... or at least, they thought so. But Jesus declared otherwise.

Jesus said to Jairus, *"Do not ________, only ________"* (v. 36). What is the significance of the word "*only*" in this verse? What might this tell us about our own faith and our own ability to experience healing in Christ?

When Jesus arrived at Jairus' house, He told the mourners that the girl was *"not dead but sleeping"* (v. 39). Some think perhaps Jesus spoke literally here and the girl was in a coma, yet many scholars believe He spoke prophetically, revealing that the girl *was* completely dead — but only for the time being. In verse 41, when Jesus said "*arise,*" the girl woke up as alive and well as if she had never died.

Jesus proved that the unclean are made clean in His presence and that the dead come back to life by His power! How do these truths encourage you today? How might you spiritually "reach out" or "wake up" in response to these scriptures?

DAY 12

MARK 6:1-13

Jesus was rejected in His hometown and sent out the 12 to preach and heal.

Hebrews 11:1 says, "*Now faith is the assurance of things hoped for, the conviction of things not seen.*" We saw this firsthand in yesterday's reading as Jairus and the bleeding woman both *hoped for* a miracle, placing their *faith* in Jesus to do what physicians could only try and fail to do. And when they believed for big things — impossible things — Jesus healed.

Today's reading offers a sharp contrast to these examples of bold faith. In Mark 6, the people from Jesus' hometown expressed cynical unbelief.

According to Matthew 2:23, what was Jesus' hometown? Locate and circle it on the map on Page 13. (Note that this is the "*hometown*" referenced in Mark 6:1, the place where Jesus spent most of His early life, even though He was *born* in Bethlehem.)

In Mark 6:2-3, Jesus taught in a synagogue on the Sabbath before an assembly — likely a group of people He knew, even people who had watched Him grow up with His family right down the street.

List the five questions the people asked after they heard Him speak:

1. ....

2. ....

3. ....

4. ....

5. ....

Mark 6:2 tells us many were *"astonished"* by Jesus. They questioned the source of His wisdom and power, and there were only two options: Either the source was God, or like the scribes had accused in Mark 3:22, the source was demonic.[1] As the people wrestled to reach a conclusion, their questions became increasingly skeptical.

Jesus was invited to speak at this synagogue because He had become a well-known teacher. But He had not studied under another rabbi as was the custom; instead, Jesus was trained in manual labor as a carpenter (Mark 6:3), so the Nazarenes questioned His qualifications.[2] Furthermore, Jesus' family was seemingly unremarkable, and the people questioned how Jesus could be any better than His kin.

In the end, the Nazarenes *"took offense"* (v. 3) at what they saw as Jesus' lack of credentials and lowly origins. Their perception of His ordinary background blinded them from seeing the extraordinary Messiah standing before them with all authority and power.

Read Mark 6:4-6. What did Jesus say and do in response to the Nazarenes' unbelief?

When verse 4 states that Jesus *"could do no mighty work"* in Nazareth, it's important to understand that unbelief does not limit Jesus' power. But their unbelief limited what He chose to do there on His mission. Jesus always has all power to heal, with or without anyone's faith, but merely impressing people with healings and miracles is not His goal. His goal is to build a Kingdom in which people have a relationship with God. And that relationship requires faith.

Later, in Mark 6:7-12, Jesus commissioned His 12 disciples to go out and build His Kingdom as well, which included proclaiming repentance, casting out demons, and healing the sick. But just as Jesus was rejected in Nazareth, so His disciples would encounter rejection on their journey.

Notice Jesus did not tell the 12 to coerce or threaten people into the Kingdom of God. If and when people rejected their message, what did Jesus instruct His disciples to do in Mark 6:11?

How does today's reading prepare you to spread the gospel and share your testimony even in the face of possible rejection? How does it encourage you that despite the unbelief of some, Jesus' Kingdom prevails — and you get to be a part of it?

DAY 13

MARK 6:14-29

Herod reluctantly executed John the Baptist after being manipulated by Herodias.

Whether it's an exit sign on the interstate or a caution sign on a wet floor, the purpose of a sign is to warn or point out what's coming. The rejection Jesus experienced in His hometown was a sign that pointed to greater rejection He would soon face from the Jewish people. Likewise, the suffering of John the Baptist in today's reading foreshadowed the greater suffering Jesus would endure on the cross.

John the Baptist disappeared from Mark's narrative after his arrest in Mark 1:14, and although Mark 2:18 briefly mentioned that John's disciples were fasting, we don't get the full details of what was happening with John until today's reading.

According to Mark 6:14-19, who arrested John, and why?

Here's the backstory: Herod Antipas, the ruler of Galilee and Perea, fell in love with his niece Herodias on a trip to Rome. However, the two of them were already married to other people. So Herod Antipas divorced his wife, and Herodias divorced her husband; then the two were wed. But since Herodias' first husband also happened to be Herod Antipas' brother, the new union violated Leviticus 20:21, which asserts that *"if a man takes his brother's wife, it is impurity."*[1] In defense of God's law, John verbally condemned Herod and Herodias' marriage, which infuriated Herodias so much that she wanted to kill John.

In Mark 6:20, why had Herod refrained from killing John the Baptist? How was Herod doing God's will in this situation, even if he didn't know it?

At Herod's birthday party, the opportunity came for Herodias to put an end to John the Baptist. Her daughter Salome performed a dance for Herod and his guests, after which he was so impressed, he vowed, *"Whatever you ask me, I will give you, up to half of my kingdom"* (v. 23).

In actuality, Herod neither held the title "king" nor had the power to give up half a kingdom. The Roman Caesar had appointed him governor over a small portion of the empire, but Herod yielded to the authority of Rome. So rather than speaking literally here, Herod was using a "royal idiom" (much like the one in Esther 5:3-6) to make a public oath of generosity.[2] Salome could make any lavish request of Herod, and he would almost certainly grant it.

Read Mark 6:24-25. What did Salome request, and how did she come to this decision? Who was in control here? (Note: This can have multiple answers. There were human hands pulling strings ... but don't forget God's hand!)

Though Herod's oath to Salome was not legally binding, he lived in a culture that valued honor and loyalty; making a vow and immediately breaking it before an audience of dinner guests would have been an utter embarrassment, unthinkable for a powerful ruler.[3] With deepest grief, he honored the oath and acquiesced to Salome's request.

Now reread Mark 6:14-16. When Herod heard about Jesus and His *"miraculous powers,"* what did he mistakenly believe?

How did Herod's words unwittingly become a sign pointing toward the truth of Ephesians 1:19-21? What does this teach us about God's sovereignty?

Herod's violence against John reminds us that proclaiming the Word of God can be dangerous. John and Jesus' other disciples faced more than just rejection — they could face execution! And many of them someday would die for their faith.

But John's death did not silence the message of God's Kingdom, nor would any execution orchestrated by rulers or religious authorities ever choke out the growth of this "mustard seed" (Mark 4:30-32). Through Jesus, the Kingdom was and is still surely coming.

COMPARE AND CONTRAST

JOHN AND JESUS

John the Baptist was not just a follower of Jesus; he was a forerunner of the Messiah. In some ways, John's life and death served as a preview of what would happen to Jesus in the later chapters of Mark's Gospel narrative.[1]

JOHN THE BAPTIST	JESUS THE MESSIAH
Called people to repentance and proclaimed the Kingdom of God (Mark 1:4).	Called people to repentance and proclaimed the Kingdom of God (Mark 1:15).
Baptized people with water (Mark 1:4).	Baptizes people with the Holy Spirit (Mark 1:8; Acts 2:4).
Rebuked immorality, like Herod's unlawful marriage (Mark 6:17-18).	Rebuked immorality, including religious hypocrisy (Mark 7:6-13; Mark 12:38-40), hardness of heart (Mark 10:5), and corruption in the temple (Mark 11:15-17).
Arrested by Herod Antipas (Mark 6:17-18).	Arrested by religious leaders and handed over to Pilate (Mark 14:53; Mark 15:1).
Known as a righteous man, even by his persecutors (Mark 6:20).	Known as a righteous man, even by His persecutors (Mark 15:10-14).
Executed by Herod under pressure from Herodias and Salome (Mark 6:26-28).	Executed by Pilate under pressure from the crowd and chief priests (Mark 15:15).
Died because Herod chose expedience over justice (Mark 6:26).	Died because Pilate chose expedience over justice (Mark 15:15).
Buried by disciples (Mark 6:29).	Buried by a disciple (Mark 15:46).
Herod thought John had risen from the dead (Mark 6:14-16).	Jesus *actually rose* from the dead (Mark 16:6).

DAY 14

MARK 6:30-56

Jesus fed 5,000 people, walked on water, and healed the sick.

In yesterday's reading, King Herod hosted a lavish feast in a palace for the rich and powerful. In today's reading, King Jesus provided a miraculous feast in a field for the poor and weak. The story begins in Mark 6:30 when the 12 apostles returned and rejoined Jesus after He had sent them out to preach and heal earlier in this chapter.

Read Mark 6:30-32. Why did they get on a boat? How is this situation similar to Mark 3:20?

When the boat came ashore at a "*desolate place*" (somewhere near Bethsaida, according to Luke 9:10), Jesus saw the crowd awaiting Him, *"and he had compassion on them, because they were like sheep without a shepherd"* (Mark 6:34).

This description is significant because in the Old Testament, Israel's spiritual and political leaders were often described as self-indulgent, careless, and cruel "*shepherds*" who failed God's people in the past (Ezekiel 34:2-6; Isaiah 56:11; Jeremiah 10:21; Zechariah 10:2-3). The shepherds of Israel in Jesus' earthly lifetime — like Herod, who we read about yesterday — were also failing the people once again.

But just as a good shepherd would care for his sheep, Jesus cared for this crowd in Mark 6. When the people hungered for God's Word, He taught them. When they hungered for food, He fed them.

In Mark 6:35-38, what did the disciples suggest, and how did Jesus respond?

Notice the crowd was in *"a desolate place"* (vv. 32, 35), meaning they were far away from towns and villages where the people could buy food. And when the disciples took inventory, they only had five loaves of bread and two fish. Feeding 5,000 people with so little food was humanly impossible.

But the God who had sustained the whole nation of Israel with manna in the wilderness (Exodus 16:15) could surely provide for 5,000 in this remote field — and He did! Jesus multiplied the bread and fish so *"all ate and were satisfied"* (Mark 6:42).

> Jesus, the Good Shepherd, satisfied the crowd's spiritual *and* physical needs. How does the Good Shepherd take care of your needs? In areas where you feel hunger or lack, how could you prayerfully seek God's provision like Jesus did when He *"looked up to heaven"* and prayed *"a blessing"* in Mark 6:41?

After the miracle, Jesus sent the disciples ahead of Him by boat, bid farewell to the crowd, and went to pray in solitude. By the time Jesus finished praying, the disciples were out at sea strenuously rowing against a strong headwind.

> Read Mark 6:48-52. When Jesus came to the disciples walking on the water, what did they think they were seeing? What was their reaction when *"the wind ceased"*?

In just the 27 verses of today's reading, Jesus proved Himself to be Lord of the wilderness, waters, and wind. But even after witnessing Jesus' countless miracles and performing mighty works themselves in Jesus' name, the disciples still struggled to understand the power He held. All 12 disciples were experiencing the same spiritual condition: hardened hearts.

This reminds us, too, that even faithful Christ followers can be slow to understand or respond to God. But today we have the help of the Holy Spirit — the One who dwells within us and enables us to understand God's Truth (1 Corinthians 2:12) — so our hearts can become more tender and responsive day by day.

The Apostle Paul prayed for the hearts of his fellow believers in Ephesians 1:17-20. Read the apostle's prayer, and then take a moment to pray these words over your own life or the life of someone you know.

A NOTE ON BETHSAIDA

Mark 6:45 tells us Jesus sent His disciples ahead of Him to Bethsaida — which seems a bit confusing since Luke 9:10 identifies Bethsaida as the location where Jesus fed the 5,000. How were they leaving Bethsaida to go to Bethsaida? And why did they end up in Gennesaret in Mark 6:53? Scholars have several possible explanations, including that there may have been multiple towns named Bethsaida. We might also understand these verses to mean that Jesus and His disciples were just outside of Bethsaida at first, and He then instructed them to go into the town, after which they would journey to Gennesaret.[1]

DAY 15

MARK 7:1-23

Jesus confronted the Pharisees about their traditions and taught that defilement comes from within.

Have you ever taken a road trip to see your favorite band or sports team play or to visit a friend or family member? You may be willing to travel many miles to see someone you like — but what about someone you don't like? You'd probably just stay home.

Nonetheless, in today's reading, the scribes who we last saw in Mark 3 traveled from Jerusalem once again to see Jesus, and along with the Pharisees, they leveled criticism at Him and His disciples. Jesus had already corrected their views on sinners, fasting, and the Sabbath (Mark 2:15-3:6), and now He would correct even more of their misinterpretations.[1]

In Mark 7:5, the scribes and Pharisees picked a fight with Jesus about hand-washing. To the Hebrews, this was not a matter of hygiene so much as ritual and ceremonial purity.[2] On Day 1 of this study, we learned about ceremonial washings that the Old Testament imposed primarily upon priests (but even then, only during temple services, after touching something dead, or before eating sacrifices). These laws were not about ordinary mealtimes (Exodus 30:17-21; Exodus 40:12; Leviticus 15:5-11). However, *extra washings* became more widely practiced by first-century religious leaders, who then attempted to impose them on all Jews.[3] And they must have been effective in their imposing — because Mark wrote that *"the Pharisees* ***and all the Jews*** *do not eat unless they wash their hands properly, holding to the tradition"* (Mark 7:3, emphasis added).

Yet in His response to the Pharisees, Jesus quoted Isaiah 29:13 and called the men "*hypocrites*" in Mark 7:6-7, using the Greek word *hypokrites*. This was a word for theatre performers who wore masks to play various character roles.[4]

Knowing this definition of *hypokrites,* what did Jesus imply about the scribes and Pharisees and their cleanness?

Jesus rebuked the religious leaders for upholding human traditions over God's commandments. It was honorable for them to study and interpret God's law, but they created *more rules* in the *"tradition of men"* to which Jesus referred (v. 8). The Pharisees believed their spoken or written traditions were as authoritative as Scripture. They believed the Torah declared *what* God's laws were while their additional writings and commentaries prescribed *how* to obey. Unfortunately, their traditions shifted attention away from the original intent of the law and even created loopholes that allowed people to violate the commandments of God.[5]

According to Mark 7:10-12, what loophole did people use so that they did not have to take care of their aging parents? Which of God's commandments did this allow people to break? (Hint: Flip over to Exodus 20:12.)

What are some loopholes Christians might use today to avoid righteous living? What loopholes are you personally tempted by?

To further make His point, Jesus addressed the crowd with a parable in Mark 7:15. Rather than addressing the matter of unclean hands, how did Jesus shift the conversation to redefine purity altogether?

Jesus' words puzzled His disciples, so He explained: Purity is not just external. It's internal. It's not really about unclean hands or unclean food but *"the things that come out of a person"* (Mark 7:15). Jesus shifted the focus from hands to stomach to heart.

Read Mark 7:20-23. What *"evil things"* did Jesus list that can come *"out of the heart"*?

1.	8.
2.	9.
3.	10.
4.	11.
5.	12.
6.	13.
7.	

The Kingdom of Jesus is "*not a matter of eating and drinking but of righteousness and peace and joy in the Holy Spirit*" (Romans 14:17). This means uncleanliness is a matter of the heart, not just ritual. A person can wash their hands, eat special foods, and follow every regulation and rite ... but still be unclean. The Pharisees believed their clean hands were a sign of piety while in fact they were *far* from God. Their hands were clean, but their hearts were filthy.

In the end, obeying laws does not produce good hearts. Good hearts produce obedience to God's Law. But Mark 7:21-22 isn't just a list of long-ago Pharisees' sins ... In some way, we can all see ourselves in it. So where do we get the good hearts we need to truly love and obey God?

Read Ezekiel 36:26-27. What does it say about the source of a *"new heart"*? How does Jesus fulfill this prophecy?

WEEK 3

WEEKEND REFLECTION & PRAYER

HE REGARDS THE DISREGARDED

Sometimes we may feel unseen and unimportant in our marriages, homes, friendships, or jobs, but even when it feels like no one else cares about us, we can rest assured that *Jesus does.* As testified in the Gospel of Mark, Jesus sees people who everyone else overlooks, and He cares for people who society considers insignificant.

In Mark 6:34, Jesus "*saw a great crowd, and he had compassion on them, because they were like sheep without a shepherd.*" But He didn't just minister to massive crowds; in Mark 5, He also showed personal compassion to individuals. Women and children, especially those with illnesses, were consigned to the lower levels of the first-century societal hierarchy — but Jesus challenged social norms when He healed a sick woman with a bleeding disorder and brought a young girl back to life. To the world, these two people meant little to nothing. To Jesus, they meant everything. They were worth His time, His care, and His healing.

Whatever prayer is on your heart today, know that it is not insignificant to God. As much as Jesus cared for the people He encountered when He walked the earth, He cares for you. He sees you, He knows what you need, and it matters to Him because *you* matter to Him.

PRAYER

Heavenly Father, You see me and You care about me, even when it feels like no one else does. Please heal and restore every part of my life that needs Your powerful touch. You are the Good Shepherd, and I trust You to meet my needs and care for me each and every day of my life. In Jesus' name, amen.

NOTES

NOTES

WEEK FOUR

DAY 16

MARK 7:24-37

Jesus healed a deaf man and a gentile girl, showing that His mercy extends beyond Israel.

Last week's Bible study revealed that the Pharisees believed the world would recognize them as God's people because they kept the Sabbath, ate "clean" foods, and washed their hands, cups, and pots. And they were right that God calls His people to be set apart as recognizably holy (Deuteronomy 7). But God's laws weren't *just* meant to serve as a boundary separating His people from their pagan counterparts. And God's boundaries were *never* meant to choke out love.[1]

In today's reading, Jesus' love and grace spilled over and crossed legalistic boundaries. The passage starts while Jesus was in the gentile region of Tyre (which you can locate on the map on Page 13), and a woman fell at his feet.

In Mark 7:26, what did she beg Jesus to do?

Verse 26 tells us this woman was *"Syrophoenician by birth,"* meaning she was from Syria but was culturally Greek, likely worshipping the Greek pantheon of gods. And while we might not expect a pagan woman to have much faith in Jesus, she demonstrated both persistence and humility before Him.

How did Jesus respond to the woman in verse 27? Write down any questions you have about His wording. (For instance: Was He telling a parable? If so, why? What is "*children's bread*"?) Take a moment to ponder this on your own before you keep reading the rest of today's study.

Interestingly, unlike the Jewish disciples who often needed further instruction to understand Jesus' parables, this gentile woman understood His words right away. The "*bread*" represented God's blessings and provision, and Jesus said feeding His "*children*," the Jews, would take precedence over feeding the gentiles, or "*dogs*."

In the regions of first-century Israel, dogs were not pets — they were wild animals and scavengers (Exodus 22:31; 1 Kings 14:11). To call someone a "dog" was usually a grave insult.[2] Some rabbinic literature likened gentiles to dogs because of their immorality.[3] So when this woman heard Jesus' analogy likening her to a dog, she could have taken offense and left infuriated ... but instead, she was not deterred.[4] Something must have told her Jesus wasn't like those other rabbis.

She countered Jesus' response with a Greek view of dogs, which were domesticated animals in some households: *"Even the dogs under the table eat the children's crumbs"* (Mark 7:28). She knew that she was undeserving and that the Jews were the first recipients of God's blessings, but she was content even to be like a little dog under Jesus' table, so long as she still got a bit of God's bread.[5] She humbled herself for just a crumb of Jesus' power ... which would be no crumb at all.

What can we learn from the Syrophoenician woman's humility and Jesus' response in Mark 7:29-30? What's one way you can follow her example of seeking Jesus even when His teachings may be challenging to receive? (See also James 4:6.)

After this, Jesus continued to travel through gentile regions, first going north to Sidon and then southeast to the Decapolis. There He healed a man who was deaf, or *kophos* in Greek. This word only occurs once in the New Testament, here in Mark 7:32. It also appears once in the Greek translation of the Old Testament (called the Septuagint); we find it in Isaiah 35, a prophecy describing the glories that await the people of God when His Kingdom is fully established.

What does Isaiah 35:5-6 say will happen ...

- To the blind? ____________________
- To the deaf? ____________________
- To the lame? ____________________
- To the mute? ____________________

How did Jesus fulfill this prophecy in Mark 7:32-37? At the same time, since we know not all people will experience physical healing on earth, what future fulfillments of this prophecy are still to come in heaven?

The deaf man in today's reading, along with all the people Jesus healed and restored during His ministry on earth, eventually died. Like us, they lived in a fallen world where death was a present reality. But Jesus' miracles give us snapshots of His everlasting Kingdom — glimpses of a future restoration when joy and peace will be our eternal reality.[6] And Jesus' care for gentiles in Tyre and the Decapolis was an early indication that this present and future Kingdom is for *everyone* who will believe in Christ.

THE "ALREADY AND NOT YET"

KINGDOM OF GOD

Psalm 90:2 is one of many scriptures that praise God as King *"from everlasting to everlasting."* This means God's reign has always been established, is already here now, and will endure forever. Yet in some ways, we are still waiting for His Kingdom to come. How can both be true at the same time?

GOD'S REIGN IN THE PRESENT

We read in Mark 1:15 that Jesus began His ministry by announcing, *"The kingdom of God is at hand."* Later, Jesus' resurrection and ascension confirmed His enthronement as Lord, and the Kingdom became a present spiritual reality for believers (Acts 2:33-36). His death on the cross broke the bondage of sin, and as Colossians 1:13 says, *"[God] has delivered us from the domain of darkness and transferred us to the kingdom of his beloved Son."* The phrase *"has delivered"* means we are living in the Kingdom right now.

GOD'S REIGN IN THE FUTURE

Although we are already transferred into God's Kingdom, it has not yet been revealed in its full glory. The Kingdom will be consummated (brought to its perfect and complete reality) in the future: *"When the Son of Man comes in his glory, and all the angels with him, then he will sit on his glorious throne"* to judge the world, delivering final justice to unbelievers and inviting believers to *"inherit the kingdom"* He has prepared for us (Matthew 25:31-46).[1]

As for now, we live in the tension of the "already and not yet," experiencing the presence of God through the Holy Spirit who dwells in us and eagerly awaiting the day when we will meet Jesus face-to-face and dwell with Him forever.[2]

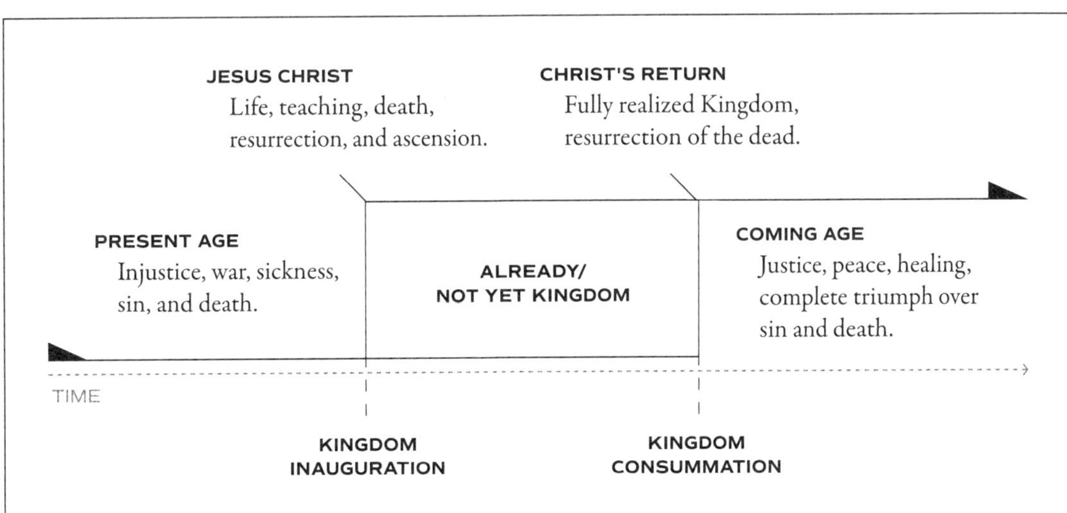

DAY 17

MARK 8:1-21

Jesus fed 4,000 people and warned His disciples about spiritual blindness and unbelief.

In John 6:35, Jesus called Himself "*the bread of life,*" saying, "*Whoever comes to me shall not hunger, and whoever believes in me shall never thirst.*" He is our ultimate spiritual provision. And the word "*whoever*" reminds us this is not just a promise for the Jewish people! In Mark 7:27, Jesus also said the "*bread*" of His blessings and provisions was available to gentiles.

Jesus even gave *literal bread* in today's reading, providing for a 4,000-person crowd in gentile territory. Some scholars point out that the location of this miracle is not specifically stated in Mark 8, but there are two major clues that Jesus was still in gentile territory: First, the text says nothing about Jesus traveling back to Galilee until *after* the miracle occurred (v. 10). Second, Jesus said in verse 3 that many in the crowd had come to Him from *"far away,"* or *makrothen*, a word commonly used in the Greek translation of the Old Testament to refer to gentile lands.[1]

> Read Mark 8:1-3. Why did Jesus have compassion on the crowd? How does this compare to Mark 6:34? (And why might it be significant that His response to *both* crowds, one Jewish and one gentile, was the same?)

We might expect that the disciples would have anticipated another miracle here. After all, they had already witnessed Jesus provide ample food for an even larger crowd with only five loaves and two fish. But their anxious response in Mark 8 was similar to their earlier response in Galilee.

And again, Jesus showed them that they did not need to worry — He multiplied bread and fish and provided enough food that all *"ate and were satisfied,"* with leftovers to spare (Mark 8:8). Again, this divine provision pointed backward to the manna God gave the Israelites in the wilderness, but it pointed forward too. Isaiah 25:6-8 prophesies of a messianic banquet in which God will someday prepare a feast for all His people and put an end to death and suffering.

When Jesus provided these two separate feasts of bread and fish in Mark 6 and Mark 8, He revealed that His Kingdom is a place where believers from *all* nations — both Jew and gentile — will be welcome at His table.

After Jesus left and went to Dalmanutha (see the map on Page 13), the Pharisees approached Him again. What were they asking for in Mark 8:11-13? Especially considering that they had already witnessed many miracles from Jesus, what did their demand indicate about their faith?

In Mark 8:14-16, Jesus' disciples continued worrying about bread. What warning did Jesus give? How did this reveal what they should *actually* be concerned about?

Yeast or leaven was a common metaphor for corruption because it only takes a small amount to permeate bread dough.[2] In the ancient world, a piece of the previous week's dough was stored and used for the next batch, and juices were added to promote fermentation (think of a "sourdough starter" today). But the yeast could easily become tainted, and baking with tainted dough would not only affect one loaf but also corrupt the next batch.[3]

Based on the context of Mark 8:15, the "*leaven of the Pharisees and the leaven of Herod,*" which also put Jesus' disciples at risk of corruption, was *unbelief in spite of evidence*.[4] Like the Israelites in the wilderness who worried about their next meal even after God provided manna (Exodus 16:18-20), the disciples panicked about their insufficient bread supply — even after Jesus miraculously fed multitudes. It was as if they could not remember what their own eyes had seen (Mark 8:18)!

Scholar David E. Garland writes, "If the disciples lift their eyes from their searching for bread, they will see that God provides them with all the food they need in Jesus."[5] The same applies to us today. When we are anxious and searching and striving to meet our own needs, we can instead lift our eyes and recognize that God is our Provider.

What other biblical accounts or personal experiences remind you that God provides? If you're not sure where to start, read Genesis 22:8-14 and 2 Peter 1:11, and then keep adding and praying through any other examples God brings to mind:

DAY 18

MARK 8:22-38

Jesus healed a blind man, predicted His own death, and called His followers to self-denial.

If you wear glasses or contacts, you might remember the first time you ever looked through prescription lenses. Suddenly, trees' leaves were sharper, faces clearer, and the whole world came into focus.

The disciples often failed to see Jesus' power and provision, and they struggled to recognize His ultimate purpose. On two separate occasions while the disciples wrestled with understanding, Jesus questioned, "*Do you not see[?]*" (Mark 7:18; Mark 8:18). In some ways they were spiritually blind. But in today's reading, Jesus demonstrated His power to heal blindness.

> In Mark 8:22-26, a man who was physically blind was brought to Jesus in Bethsaida. How did Jesus heal him in an unexpected way? How was this particular healing different from past healings? (For instance, the bleeding woman and Jairus' daughter in Mark 5 were healed instantly when they touched Jesus or He touched them.)

Why the two stages of healing? It's not like Jesus tried to heal and failed halfway through. He was demonstrating something to us. Perhaps one explanation is that the disciples would also experience two stages of revelation. They had already received blessings from Jesus, but they still had blurry vision when it came to spiritual insight.[1] The disciples would need a second touch from Jesus to fully see and understand who He is and the Kingdom He brings.

> Later, as Jesus and His disciples were traveling to the villages of Caesarea Philippi, He asked them, "*Who do people say that I am?*" (Mark 8:27). How did the disciples answer in verse 28?

At this time, the prophets of the Old Testament had ceased; after Malachi in the 400s B.C., God didn't send any new prophets to speak in His name until John the Baptist. So to confess that Jesus was a prophet was radical. But even still, it was not radical enough.[2]

The question of Jesus' identity has been an overarching theme from the opening verse of Mark's Gospel, and it reaches a climax in this moment as Jesus shifted from the opinion of "*people*" (v. 27) to that of His own disciples, asking, *"Who do **you** say that I am?"* (v. 29, emphasis added). As readers, we wonder, *Will the disciples finally begin to see who Jesus is?*

Peter answered, *"You are the Christ"* (v. 29).

The term "*Christ*" has not been used in Mark's Gospel since the opening verse, but here a disciple at last recognized Jesus as the Messiah! Even so, Peter was still half-blind about what kind of Messiah Jesus would be. The idea of the Messiah or Christ had taken on nationalistic and militaristic connotations in Israel — many Jews believed He would free their nation politically and crush Israel's enemies. Peter probably had similar expectations.[3] His answer was right, but his understanding was wrong.

In Mark 8:31, Jesus didn't talk about a future in which He would crush Rome; He instead talked about Himself being crushed. In what ways would the "*Son of Man*" suffer? What would happen after three days?

The disciples would have expected the Son of Man to be exalted based on Daniel 7:13-14, but they didn't necessarily expect Him to *suffer*. They had scriptures like Isaiah 53:5 that prophesied about God's suffering Servant: *"He was pierced for our transgressions; he was crushed for our iniquities ..."* But in Jewish history and literature, the suffering Servant of Isaiah was not closely associated with the future messianic King.[4] This idea would have been foreign to the disciples, which was likely why Peter rebuked Jesus in Mark 8:32.

How did Jesus respond to Peter in verse 33? Does anything about this response surprise you? Why or why not?

A good disciple gets behind his master, and that's where Peter needed to be — following behind Jesus. Jesus then demanded three things of all His disciples in Mark 8:34:

1. *"Let him deny himself."* Disciples push aside personal ambitions, setting aside their desires for the sake of God's higher purpose.

2. *"Take up his cross."* Even before Jesus' crucifixion, He referenced this cruel Roman form of execution to indicate that true disciples are willing to suffer for Him, even unto death.

3. *"Follow me."* Disciples walk in the way of the Master, actively aligning their lives with His.

Based on these callings from Jesus, how are you doing in your discipleship? In which areas do you need to see Him more clearly or follow Him more faithfully? Take a moment to reflect below, and then write one step you can take this week to move toward self-denying, cross-carrying, Jesus-following faith.

Finally, Jesus issued a warning in verse 38 about what will happen to those who are "*ashamed*" of Him and His words. What might this have meant to first-century Christian readers who were living under the threat of the Roman Emperor Nero's persecution? (See Page 11 for a refresher on this context.) What does it mean to you?

WHY DID JESUS HEAL WITH SPIT?

In Mark 8:22-26, Jesus used "spit" *when healing a blind man, which may seem unusual or even disrespectful to modern readers. Yet some scholars suggest the use of spit was a symbol emphasizing the tangible and personal nature of Jesus' ministry: He healed with a substance administered from His own body as well as* "laid his hands" *on the blind man. Others note that in the cultural context of the time, spit was sometimes believed to have medicinal properties, so Jesus' actions may have communicated to those watching Him that healing was taking place.*

DAY 19

MARK 9:1-13

Jesus was transfigured before three disciples, confirming His identity as God's Son.

When God stepped into human history to redeem humankind, 12 disciples had front-row seats. But at first, they didn't understand what was unfolding before them. Although Peter recognized Jesus' identity in Mark 8:29, his understanding of "*the Christ*" was incomplete, and his expectation of the coming Kingdom was flawed.

In Mark 9:1, what promise did Jesus make regarding the Kingdom? How do you think this made His disciples feel?

Jesus said His Kingdom would "*come with power*" in the near future — so near that even some of the people listening to His words would see it happen (Mark 9:1). But to what event was Jesus specifically referring? Scholars don't always agree. Some interpret this as a reference to Jesus' Transfiguration, which happened soon afterward in Mark 9:2-9, while others interpret the Kingdom's coming as a reference to His resurrection, which His disciples witnessed later. Since biblical prophecies often have both "near" and "far" fulfillments, one scholar argues that Jesus could have been referring to a series of future events, including His Transfiguration, death, resurrection, and ascension, then extending to Pentecost and beyond.[1]

What we do know is that six days later, Jesus went up on a mountain with Peter, James, and John. These were the first three disciples Jesus called (Mark 3:15-17), the only three Jesus took with Him when He raised Jairus' daughter from the dead (Mark 5:37), and the three Jesus chose to witness His Transfiguration.

The Greek root word for "*transfigured*" in Mark 9:2 is *metamorphoo,* which means "change" or "transform" and is also the origin of the English word "metamorphosis." In both biblical Greek and modern English, it refers to a *radical* change. In the presence of His "inner circle" of disciples, Jesus changed in appearance, remaining a human being yet now revealing His glorious divinity.[2]

How else do the following passages describe Jesus' appearance at the Transfiguration?

- Mark 9:3: ____________________
- Luke 9:29: ____________________
- Matthew 17:2: ____________________

After Jesus was transfigured, there appeared two prominent figures from Israel's history, Moses and Elijah, both of whom had also experienced God's glorious presence on a mountain (Exodus 19-20; 1 Kings 19). Both of these men served God faithfully and followed His will during their lifetimes.[3] And now the divine plan God had begun through these Old Testament saints was entering a new era: a new covenant in Jesus.

Next, for the second time in Mark's narrative, a voice came from heaven. Let's compare and contrast Mark 1:11 and Mark 9:7.

VERSE	MESSAGE FROM GOD	RECIPIENT(S) OF MESSAGE	PURPOSE OF MESSAGE
MARK 1:11			
MARK 9:7			

In Mark 9:9, on the way down the mountain, what order did Jesus give the three disciples? How does Jesus' command here shed more light on His reason for keeping the "messianic secret"?

Even Jesus' own disciples would not fully understand His true identity and significance until after His death and resurrection — so the events of the Transfiguration would have surely been misinterpreted by others if the disciples had shared them right away.[4] It already puzzled Peter, James, and John that the Son of Man would have to suffer and die since they expected Elijah to *"come first to restore all things"* (Mark 9:11-13).

This expectation was based on Malachi 4:5-6. What did this prophecy say about Elijah?

In Mark 9:13, what did Jesus say about Elijah? To whom was Jesus referring? (Hint: Read Matthew's parallel account of this conversation in Matthew 17:11-13.)

To clarify, Jesus was not calling John the Baptist a "reincarnation" of Elijah, as though Elijah's soul was reborn in John's body. Reincarnation is not a biblical idea. Plus, the disciples had *just seen* Elijah in his heavenly body standing on a mountain with Jesus! So they knew Elijah and John were different people. But Luke 1:17 clarifies that John prophesied *"in the spirit and power of Elijah,"* fulfilling a similar role as a forerunner to the Messiah. John's suffering and death as an "Elijah" was also a prelude to Jesus' suffering and death on the cross.

With this, Jesus warned His disciples they would soon see His humiliation ... however, the Transfiguration also gave them a small glimpse of His future exaltation.

DAY 20

MARK 9:14-29

Jesus healed a boy with an unclean spirit the disciples could not cast out.

"No problem. That will be easy." If we've done something successfully many times, we might make a claim like this, expecting to succeed again — but sometimes we fail. Then the situation becomes frustrating and confusing.

In today's reading, Jesus' disciples experienced unexpected failure. While Jesus, Peter, James, and John were on the mountain of Transfiguration, a man asked the remaining disciples to expel an evil spirit from his son. Even though they had expelled demons in the past (Mark 3:14-15) and likely assumed they could do so again whenever they wished ... this time, they failed.

When Jesus came down from the mountain and heard the commotion, He said, *"O faithless generation, how long am I to be with you?"* (Mark 9:19). Jesus' time on earth would soon end, and it would be His disciples' mission to spread the gospel after He was gone. Yet the disciples belonged to a *"faithless generation"* — and even in His brief absence, their own faith had already failed.[1] What would happen when He left earth for a much longer period of time?

What sustains your faith today, in your own generation, as you await Jesus' return?

When the evil spirit in Mark 9:20 saw Jesus, it threw the boy into seizure-like convulsions. The situation seemed dire. The evil spirit had tormented the boy from childhood, and up to this point, no one had been able to expel it and heal him.

The boy's father said to Jesus, *"If you can do anything ... help us"* (v. 22). Based on Jesus' response in verse 23, what does the man's word choice here tell us about his faith?

Jesus' point was not to say that anything is possible if you have *enough* faith. It is not the *amount* of faith that matters. Elsewhere, Jesus said just a tiny mustard seed of faith in Him can move mountains (Matthew 17:20)! It's the *object* of our faith that makes all things possible.[2] The God in whom we trust has the power to do impossible things.

Yet failed exorcism attempts had dashed the father's hopes, and his faith was wavering. While even this could not prevent Jesus from acting, it did highlight the man's deep need for help in believing. The absence of faith is known to hinder miracles (Mark 6:3-5), but we also serve a God who is graciously willing to answer prayers like the one this man exclaimed in Mark 9:24: *"I believe; help my unbelief!"*

How might this prayer help you when your own faith feels weak? What would it look like for God to answer this prayer in your life?

When Jesus expelled the unclean spirit from the boy, the disciples wondered why their attempts had failed. In Mark 9:29, what did Jesus say? What does this reveal about the power and necessity of prayer?

The disciples likely failed to cast out the spirit because their faith was misdirected toward themselves rather than rightly directed at God. Perhaps they had begun to think their authority to cast out demons came from some kind of status they had earned as Jesus' disciples or the techniques they learned from Him — but in fact, they had no power apart from God.[3] The solution was prayer. Because properly directed faith in God is a product of consistent communication with God.

Below, close by writing a prayer to confess the areas of your life where your faith tends to waver. Ask God to help you overcome any unbelief, not just today but consistently moving forward.

WEEK 4

WEEKEND REFLECTION & PRAYER

WHEN WE DON'T UNDERSTAND WHAT GOD IS DOING

In this week's readings from Mark, Jesus' disciples were spiritually blind in some ways. Even after walking with the Master, witnessing many miracles, and receiving private instruction, there was much they still did not see and understand. When Jesus plainly told them of His upcoming suffering, rejection, and death, Peter even rebuked Jesus in Mark 8:31-33; such a horrible fate did not align with Peter's personal expectations of the Messiah.

But let's not judge the disciples too harshly ... because even when we have followed Jesus for a long time, moments arise when we can't grasp what God is doing or when our current circumstances do not match our expectations.

There are seasons of disappointment when we wonder, *What now, God?*
There are seasons of waiting when we wonder, *What's next, God?*
There are seasons of turmoil when we cry out, *Why, God?*
No matter how hard we squint and strain our eyes, His plan just doesn't make sense to us.

In those moments, when we struggle with doubt that begins to creep in, let our prayers be like that of the father who cried to Jesus, *"Help my unbelief!"* (Mark 9:24). On the other side of this powerless, imperfect prayer was a miracle from a powerful, perfect God. May our hearts be reminded that He has the power to transform our circumstances far beyond our comprehension and that He will somehow work it all out for good (Ephesians 3:20; Romans 8:28).

PRAYER

Heavenly Father, when I question everything, please help me to walk by faith and not by sight. Open my eyes to Your unlimited power and goodness, and when I doubt, Lord, help my unbelief! Help me to let go of my own expectations and lean into Your plan. Your ways are always higher. In Jesus' name, amen.

NOTES

NOTES

WEEK FIVE

DAY 21

MARK 9:30-50

Jesus predicted His death again and taught about humility and temptation.

In last week's reading, even though Jesus spoke plainly, the disciples struggled to understand what He meant when He warned about the Son of Man's future death and resurrection. Again in today's reading, Jesus warned them that the Son of Man would be killed, *"and when he is killed, after three days he will rise"* (Mark 9:31). Again, they missed the meaning of it all.

Jesus' disciples would have been familiar with Old Testament scriptures like Daniel 12:2-3, which prophesies an end-time resurrection of the dead when God will judge all people, raising *"those who sleep in the dust of the earth ... some to everlasting life, and some to shame and everlasting contempt."* So the 12 might have expected a final resurrection for all people, but the concept of an individual resurrection after three days, as Jesus described in Mark 9:31, would have been entirely unfamiliar to them.[1]

> According to Mark 9:32, how did the disciples deal with their confusion? Have you ever responded to Jesus in this way? Why or why not?

The disciples also "*kept silent*" in verse 34, trying to avoid a convicting question Jesus asked them as they passed again through Galilee and into Capernaum. This time, rather than performing miracles as they traveled, Jesus focused His attention on teaching the disciples and preparing them for what would soon come. But the 12 were arguing among themselves, disputing who was the greatest.

> In verses 35-37, what did Jesus say they must do if they wanted to "*be first*"? How does this demonstrate that engaging in prideful disputes is the very thing that would *disqualify* someone from being the first and greatest in Jesus' Kingdom?

Jockeying for higher rank is not the way of Christ — the way of His Kingdom is humble service. To teach this, Jesus took a small child in His arms and showed the disciples an example of *who* to serve. In Ancient Near Eastern society, children had no power, no status, and few rights. Jesus said the first and greatest disciple is the one willing to serve people like this: those who have no official titles, no social influence, and no political importance.[2] As the ultimate model of this very concept, the Son of God Himself would soon go to the cross as a suffering Servant, laying His life down for many.

If we are to follow Jesus well, our hearts need to be willing to humbly serve others. In what ways do you serve others in your life? How could you begin or seek new ways to do so?

John also told Jesus about a man casting out demons in His name in Mark 9:38-41. Why did the disciples tell the man to stop? How might this further reveal their spirit of superiority rather than Christlike humility?

The disciples' reaction was ironic because they *themselves* had recently failed at expelling an evil spirit in Mark 9:18! Yet this man was successfully driving out demons in the name of Jesus. Even though he was not one of the 12, he recognized Jesus' power at least to some extent and was therefore an ally, not an enemy. In the coming days of persecution, acts of benevolence toward Jesus' disciples would be few and far between, and they would surely appreciate such allies who might show them basic kindness or give them *"a cup of water to drink"* (v. 41).[3]

Instead of focusing on evil outside of their circle, Jesus redirected the disciples to evil that might be lurking within them, saying in Mark 9:43-48 that if their own hand, foot, or eye should cause them to stumble, they should *"cut it off."* Jesus was not speaking literally — He certainly did not expect the disciples or anyone else to mutilate themselves. But He was using hyperbole, or deliberate exaggeration, to make a forceful point.

In your own words, what point was Jesus making in this passage? (See also Romans 8:13 and Colossians 3:5.)

What compromises, bad influences, unhealthy habits, or sinful temptations might you need to "cut off" in your life this week? Why is it important that this sacrifice comes with the promise of *"enter[ing] the kingdom of God"* (Mark 9:47)?

WHO EXACTLY IS "FOR US"?

At first glance, Jesus' words in Mark 9:40 — "for the one who is not against us is for us" *— may seem to contradict His words in Matthew 12:30, where He said,* "Whoever is not with me is against me." *But the context of each statement shows that they actually complement each other. In the first example, Jesus was teaching His disciples not to be narrow or jealous, emphasizing that anyone genuinely working in His name was on His side, even if they were outside the 12. In the example from Matthew, Jesus was warning His opponents that neutrality toward Him is impossible. Those who reject Jesus, or even those who are indifferent to Him, stand against Him. Taken together, these two sayings show the importance of both: 1) generosity in our judgment of fellow believers and 2) seriousness in our allegiance to Christ.*

DAY 22

MARK 10:1-16

Jesus taught about marriage and divorce, and He welcomed little children.

Jesus' Galilean ministry concluded in last week's reading, and in Mark 10, Jesus now traveled to Judea and across the Jordan, possibly into the province of Perea. (You can trace this route on the map on Page 13.) Here the Pharisees approached Jesus again, this time meaning to test Him by asking about divorce.

Especially if they were in Perea — a province under Herod Antipas' rule — divorce was a potentially dangerous subject. Remember that John the Baptist lost his life for speaking out against Herod's divorce and remarriage (Mark 6:17-27).[1]

What question did the Pharisees ask in Mark 10:2? The book of Matthew records the same question in greater detail. What phrase does Matthew 19:3 add, and why might this be important?

Jesus answered their question with His own question in Mark 10:3, saying, *"What did Moses command you?"* Then the Pharisees referenced Deuteronomy 24:1-4.

Based on Deuteronomy 24:1, a man was justified in divorcing his wife *"because he has found some"* what? What do you think this means?

In Hebrew, the word for "*indecency*" can also be translated as "nakedness" or "shame." It doesn't refer specifically to adultery (which was actually punishable by death, not just divorce), but it implies sinful behavior. How do you think this ambiguity may have affected people's interpretations of Deuteronomy 24 in ancient Israel?

The Pharisees were themselves divided on what constituted divorce-worthy behavior. Two major interpretations existed:

1. The House of Shammai argued that moral fault (adultery or failure to observe Jewish marriage laws) was the only acceptable reason for divorce.

2. The House of Hillel argued that anything causing a husband embarrassment or annoyance was grounds for divorce.[2] A man could divorce his wife if she burnt the toast or even if he found someone else more attractive.[3]

A Jewish woman, on the other hand, technically did not have the legal right to divorce her husband even if he was unfaithful. A man having relations with an unmarried woman was not considered adulterous; some wrongly reasoned that adultery only "counted" if one married man violated another man's marriage by sleeping with his wife.[4]

However, even in the Old Testament times, this narrow definition would not be mistaken for divine approval by those who truly knew God's heart and the spirit of His law. Any unfaithfulness in marriage was still immoral and contrary to God's design. Even if human courts overlooked such sin, God Himself holds both men and women accountable, and His justice prevails whether in this life or the next. Malachi 2:14-16 makes clear that godly marriage is a "*covenant*," and God says, *"Do not be faithless."*

According to Mark 10:6-9, what was God's original intent for marriage, established at the time of creation?

In Mark 10:5, Jesus said, *"Because of your ______________ of __________ [Moses] wrote you this commandment"* about divorce. As God's commands reveal human brokenness and offer us His better way to live, what do they also tell us about *His* heart?

In a perfect world, all marriages would be healthy and permanent. But the heartbreaking truth is that we live in a fallen world, and in Deuteronomy 24, God recognized that some people would dishonor their marriage covenant. Still, His law through Moses made divorce more regulated and protective than it had been before. The Mosaic law required a husband to issue a written *"certificate of divorce"* (Mark 10:4) — not dismissing his wife by simply saying the word — which would give her legal acknowledgment, some security, and protection from arbitrary abandonment.

Jesus' teaching on marriage further elevated the status of wives and women in general.[5] In Mark 10:11, Jesus declared more clearly than ever before that a *man* could be guilty of adultery *against his wife.*[6] In verses 6-9, Jesus also said *"God made them male and female"* to be equal creations, mutually responsible in the marriage union.[7] He emphasized that both husband and wife should take their marriage vows seriously.

It is clear from Jesus' teaching that God's will is for husband and wife to remain in a lifelong union. However, the New Testament also makes some exceptions for divorce, like adultery or abandonment by an unbelieving spouse (Matthew 5:32; Matthew 19:9; 1 Corinthians 7:15). And even if divorce has happened for reasons beyond these exceptions, God is *always* forgiving. He shows us love and grace no matter our marriage history. Whatever our past, He invites us to walk faithfully with Him today, tomorrow, and every day of our lives.

Let's wrap up by reading Jesus' conversation with a divorced woman in John 4:16-26. Just as He said *"let the children come to me"* in Mark 10:14, how does this conversation show Jesus' invitational posture toward all who seek Him?

DAY 23

MARK 10:17-34

Jesus challenged a rich young man, then foretold His own death and resurrection again.

In yesterday's reading, after Jesus concluded his teaching on marriage, He picked up a child and said to His disciples, "*Whoever does not receive the kingdom of God like a child shall not enter it*" (Mark 10:15). Just as a child depends on a parent to respond to their needs and ensure their well-being, we are called to abandon self-reliance and wholly depend on our heavenly Father if we truly want to live in His Kingdom.

In Mark 10:17, Jesus met a man who was seeking this Kingdom: He knelt before Jesus and asked, "*What must I do to inherit eternal life?*" This question, echoing Daniel 12:2 and the idea of ultimate salvation in God's presence, suggests the man had a clearer picture of the Kingdom of God than many of Jesus' own disciples. But sadly, he did not receive it with childlike faith.

What else do we learn about this man's age, wealth, and status from the Gospels?

- Matthew 19:22: ______
- Mark 10:22: ______
- Luke 18:18: ______

In Mark 10:19-20, when Jesus listed several of the Ten Commandments, this man claimed he had obeyed them since he was a boy. He understood and faithfully followed the requirements of the law, but there was something he still lacked — radical trust in God.

What directive did Jesus give the man in verse 21? Why is it significant that Jesus was "*looking at him*" and "*loved him*" as He gave this command?

Though the man claimed righteous living, he could not enter the Kingdom of God by his righteous deeds or his treasures alone; he had to enter like a child who owned nothing and could do nothing.[1] This man was asked to do the same as the fishermen and tax collector who left their livelihoods behind to follow Jesus (Mark 1:18-20; Mark 2:13-14). But he struggled to let go of his money and possessions.

In the rich man's case, his wealth was his first love. When he had to choose between earthly treasure and eternal life with God, he chose earthly treasure. While wealth is not necessarily evil, if we place too much confidence in financial stability and self-sufficiency, it can become a hindrance to our faith. This man's wealth became an evil thing that held him back from following Jesus. He was *so close* to the Kingdom, yet as far as we know, he missed it: *"He went away sorrowful ..."* (Mark 10:22).

How have possessions or comforts kept you from following the will of God? What would it look like for you to see the love in Jesus' eyes as He calls you to sacrifice and surrender all for Him?

Jesus followed the rich man's exit with a parable: *"It is easier for a camel to go through the eye of a needle than for a rich person to enter the kingdom of God"* (v. 25). Imagine the largest animal known in Israel trying to squeeze through the smallest conceivable hole. This image made a strong point to shock the disciples: *It's impossible.*

If a law-abiding Jewish man of high status cannot enter God's Kingdom, *"Then who can be saved?"* the disciples asked in verse 26. How did Jesus answer?

Any attempt at salvation on the basis of merit is futile because there is nothing we can do to achieve entrance into God's Kingdom. But what was impossible would soon be made possible through the life and work of Jesus: God was preparing a way for *anyone* to be saved.

In the last verses of today's reading, Jesus and His disciples were on the road to Jerusalem, the very place where Jesus would complete the work that would make salvation possible for all people.

In Mark 10:33-34, what did Jesus warn would happen to Him in Jerusalem? How does this demonstrate that any sacrifice we make to follow Jesus pales in comparison to His sacrifice for us?

DAY 24

MARK 10:35-52

Jesus corrected His disciples' selfish ambition and healed Bartimaeus.

In contrast to the rich young ruler who sought Jesus for eternal life, in today's reading, two of Jesus' disciples had a more temporal request. As Jesus was traveling to Jerusalem, the holy city and the site of God's temple, James and John seized what they thought was an opportunity to secure positions of honor and prestige in the coming Kingdom of God.

At least two other times in Mark's Gospel, Jesus had already corrected the disciples' misunderstandings of His Kingdom: near Caesarea Philippi (Mark 8:31-33), in Galilee (Mark 9:33-37), and now again on the road to Jerusalem. Yet even after hearing Jesus say He would be flogged and killed in Mark 10:34, James and John still expected Jesus to sit on an earthly throne immediately. And not only that, but they hoped He would grant them status as His crown princes.

In Mark 10:37-40, when James and John asked to sit on thrones at Jesus' right and left, how did Jesus answer? Why do you think we keep seeing Jesus answer people's questions with questions?

What is the metaphorical "*cup*" to which Jesus referred in Mark 10:38? (See Mark 14:36 and John 18:11.)

When asked to drink with Jesus, these disciples answered, *"We are able"* (Mark 10:39). They might have thought Jesus was referring to a cup of victory, or at least they were confident they could endure drinking some hardship if there was a seat of power up for grabs in the end. But God's Kingdom does not operate like earthly kingdoms. Just a few verses ago, Jesus told them the last will be first. Now Jesus further explained how His Kingdom is different from all others.

Complete the charts using Mark 10:42-44:

EARTHLY KINGDOMS	
WHO?	WHAT DO THEY DO? (AND WHY?)
"Rulers of the Gentiles"	
"Their great ones"	

GOD'S KINGDOM	
WHO?	WHAT DO THEY DO? (AND WHY?)
"Whoever would be great"	
"Whoever would be first"	

In Mark 10:45, Jesus clearly stated His purpose: *"For even the Son of Man came not to be served but to serve, and to give his life as a ransom for many."* Then He demonstrated His servant-heartedness as He and His disciples passed through Jericho, and as they were leaving, a man named Bartimaeus called out to Jesus.

Bartimaeus was blind, which in the ancient world meant he would have been entirely dependent on others for charity, guidance, and protection. Even though society considered him expendable and the crowd rebuked his cries for help in Mark 10:48, Jesus saw value in Bartimaeus. He stopped.[1] *No one is insignificant in God's Kingdom.*

Read Mark 10:49-52. How did Bartimaeus come when Jesus called for him? What did he do after Jesus healed him? How do both of these actions demonstrate faith?

Let's take a moment to compare and contrast Bartimaeus' actions with those of the rich young ruler. Both sought Jesus for help, but while the rich man clung to his treasures, Bartimaeus left behind everything — *"throwing off his cloak"* (v. 50), which was likely his only possession — and followed Jesus.

A cloak may not seem like much, but for a man in Bartimaeus' situation, it was extremely important. He would have spread out the cloak before him each day to collect alms (gifts of money), and he would have wrapped it around himself each night as a source of warmth.[2] In his past, Bartimaeus had fully depended on his cloak, but now he was putting his trust in the One who healed him.

Different from the young ruler who asked Jesus, *"What must **I do**"* (Mark 10:17), Bartimaeus accepted Jesus' offer, *"What do you want me to do **for you?**"* (Mark 10:51). What might this teach us about the unearned gift of salvation?

WHY WERE THE FOLLOWERS AFRAID?

As Jesus was going up to Jerusalem, "those who followed were afraid" *in Mark 10:32. Who are* "those" *and why were they* "afraid"*? This verse likely references followers of Jesus, and perhaps other traveling Jewish pilgrims, who may have feared that He would start a messianic war with the Romans. This would also explain the timing of James and John's request: If the two disciples were expecting imminent war in Jerusalem, it makes sense that they would want to secure their postwar positions before the battle began.[3] This interpretation also explains why Jesus specifically corrected their misunderstanding of the Messiah, the* "Son of Man," *in verse 45.*

PASSION WEEK

IN MARK'S GOSPEL

SUNDAY *PALM SUNDAY*	MONDAY	TUESDAY	WEDNESDAY
MARK 11:1-11	MARK 11:12-19	MARK 11:20-13:37	MARK 14:1-11
Jesus made His triumphal entry into Jerusalem. He briefly visited the temple, then returned to Bethany with the 12.	Jesus cursed a fruitless fig tree on the way back into Jerusalem. He cleansed the temple of corrupt merchants, then returned to Bethany again.	Jewish religious leaders tried to trap Jesus with questions. Jesus praised a widow's offering and prophesied about the destruction of the temple.	The priests, scribes, and elders plotted to kill Jesus, and Judas Iscariot joined them. Meanwhile, Jesus was anointed by a woman in Bethany.
THURSDAY *MAUNDY* THURSDAY*	**FRIDAY** *GOOD FRIDAY*	**SATURDAY** *SABBATH*	**SUNDAY** *RESURRECTION SUNDAY*
MARK 14:12-40	MARK 14:41-15:47		MARK 16:1-8
Jesus and the 12 prepared for Passover, then ate the Last Supper together, where Jesus gave new meaning to the bread and wine they shared. Afterward, they went to the Mount of Olives, and Jesus prayed in the garden of Gethsemane.	Judas betrayed Jesus, and authorities arrested Him as the other disciples fled. Jesus stood trial before the Jewish Sanhedrin, then Pilate of Rome. Found guilty of capital crimes, Jesus was beaten, crucified, and buried.	Jesus was dead. *(Jesus died in His human nature, and His body lay in the tomb. His soul was separated from it, as happens with all who die. Yet in His divine nature, He remained alive and sovereign, for God can never cease to exist.)*	Women visited Jesus' tomb, but the stone was rolled away, and an angel told them Jesus had risen from the dead and would meet them soon in Galilee.

**"Maundy" is a word for "mandate" and refers to the new commands Jesus gave His disciples at the Last Supper.*

DAY 25

MARK 11

Jesus entered Jerusalem, cleansed the temple, and confronted religious leaders.

The word "passion" comes from the Latin *passio*, meaning "suffering." Definitions of this word also include "ardent affection," "strong desire or devotion," and "fervor, ardor, or zeal."[1] All of these meanings are wrapped up together in what many Christians call "Passion Week" — the final seven days of Jesus' earthly life.

In today's reading, Jesus arrived at Jerusalem, the final stop of His ministry journey. And so begins the Passion narrative of Mark's Gospel. The city was gearing up for the Passover festival, one of three pilgrimage festivals in which Jews were to travel to Jerusalem and bring offerings to the temple.

Pilgrims traveling into the city typically completed the final stage of their pilgrimage on foot, but Jesus entered in a different manner, riding *"a colt ... on which no one has ever sat"* (Mark 11:2).[2] In the Old Testament, animals that had never been yoked were set apart for sacred purposes (Numbers 19:2; Deuteronomy 21:3; 1 Samuel 6:7).[3] And the colt Jesus called for in Mark 11 would certainly have a sacred purpose in His entrance into Jerusalem.

What did Zechariah 9:9-10 say about a coming King? How did Jesus fulfill the words of the prophet Zechariah in Mark 11:1-10?

Jesus' undeniably messianic entrance into the city stands in stark contrast to His prior attempts to maintain a low profile and keep His identity discreet (Mark 1:43-44; Mark 8:29-30). Why do you think this is? Why would Jesus draw more attention to His ministry right before His crucifixion?

As Jesus entered Jerusalem, His followers and other excited pilgrims threw garments and leafy branches on the ground before Him (similar to an event in 2 Kings 9:13 where garments were placed on the steps before a newly appointed king), and they lined the streets shouting and rejoicing.[4] But Jesus' dramatic entry was immediately followed by an anticlimactic visit to the temple in Mark 11:11. There was no priestly greeting as Jesus entered the temple courts; He just looked things over for a moment and then retired for the evening with His disciples.[5]

Yet one commentator points out that more was happening here than we might realize: Jesus did not offer prayers or sacrifices in the temple, nor did He gawk at the buildings like a tourist. When Jesus arrived, He entered *His* temple *as Lord*, and He inspected it knowing He would soon return to pronounce judgment.[6]

Read Malachi 3:1-2. What did Malachi say the Lord will be like when He comes to the temple?

While walking back to the temple the next day, Jesus was hungry and saw a fig tree in Mark 11:12-13. It was still too early in the year for figs, as fig trees produce early fruit in May or June, and Passover occurs in March or April. Even so, this tree's appearance hinted there was fruit — but when Jesus examined it, there were only leaves.

What did Jesus say about the fruitless fig tree in verse 14? How might His inspection and rebuke of the tree relate to His inspection of the temple in verse 11 followed by His rebuke in verses 15-17?

In a way, Jesus was acting out a parable here: Just as He had inspected the fig tree and found it to be fruitless, so, too, He inspected the temple and found it to be all "leaves" (outward, spiritual-looking activity) and no "fruit" (genuine spiritual growth).

How did the priests and religious teachers react to Jesus' actions in the temple in Mark 11:18? What does this reveal about the danger of clinging to power and position?

The fate of the fig tree was a symbol of judgment soon to fall on unbelieving Jerusalem.[7] Before long, the Jewish temple would be destroyed. But Jesus told His disciples to *"have faith in God"* (Mark 11:22) — because His Church, made up of believers in whom the Holy Spirit dwells, would become the *new temple* of the Lord. God's Kingdom wouldn't be like a fruitless fig tree; it would be like wild mustard spreading across the world.

> How might this idea of Church growth illuminate Jesus' reference to *"all the nations"* in Mark 11:17? In light of Jesus' comments about prayer in verses 22-24, how can you pray for the worldwide spread of His Kingdom?

A HOUSE OF PRAYER

All four Gospels record that Jesus overthrew tables and drove out corrupt merchants from the temple (Mark 11:15-17; Matthew 21:12-13; John 2:14-16; Luke 19:45-46). This may seem like an uncharacteristically aggressive or even violent act for Jesus, and so we naturally wonder ... Why?

The money changers Jesus encountered were exchanging the Roman coins for the Tyrian shekel, the currency required for the temple tax, which was due two weeks before Passover.[1] According to the Old Testament, pilgrims were not expected to bring sacrifices from far away but to bring currency to convert upon arrival in Jerusalem (Deuteronomy 14:24-25), which they would use to purchase animals for sacrifice (Ezra 7:17). The temple offered both currency exchange services and doves for purchase, neither of which was necessarily against the Word of God. The issue, therefore, was not the existence of the market but the **location** of it.[2]

After Jesus turned over the tables, He said, "*Is it not written, 'My house shall be called a house of prayer for all the nations'*?" (Mark 11:17). Commentators often find significance in the phrase "*for all the nations,*" which refers to gentile worshippers of God. Gentiles had a place in the temple (Isaiah 56:6-7), but in Jesus' day, they were restricted to the outer courts.[3] And that's exactly where the money changers and merchants were.

In the Torah, there was no law excluding gentiles specifically from the inner court. God's Word emphasized holiness distinctions between priests and laypeople but did not create an ethnic barrier in worship between Jew and gentile. In fact, foreigners who committed to follow the God of Israel were welcomed into covenant life and worship. God said, "*There shall be one law for the native and for the stranger who sojourns among you*" (Exodus 12:49). God also commanded, "*When a stranger sojourns with you in your land, you shall not do him wrong. You shall treat the stranger who sojourns with you as the native among you, and you shall love him as yourself*" (Leviticus 19:33-34).

In this sense, "The Court of Gentiles," promoting their separation, shouldn't have existed. What could have been a consecrated place for Jews and non-Jews to worship God instead was reduced to a loud, smelly bazaar where people focused on making a profit.

So why did Jesus forcefully drive out the buyers and sellers? He was demonstrating honor for God and His house and providing a place, literally and spiritually, for believing gentiles to worship the Lord.

WEEK 5

WEEKEND REFLECTION & PRAYER

RADICAL SERVANTHOOD

"What's the catch?" We often ask that question when someone has offered to freely give or do something for us — because we live in a world where payment is usually required for the goods and services we want and need. When we give our time, energy, and resources, we also generally expect something in return.

However, Jesus' idea of servanthood runs counter to this transaction-driven mindset. Servanthood requires giving to someone and expecting nothing in return — no compensation, recognition, appreciation, or reciprocation. As we heard from Jesus when we studied Mark 10:44-45 this week, *"Whoever would be first among you must be slave of all. For even the Son of Man came not to be served but to serve, and to give his life as a ransom for many."*

Servanthood also opposes the human desire to pursue superiority (Mark 10:37-43). Our world values "winners," but if we spend our lives striving to be first and greatest, we will be too blinded by self-importance to recognize the needs of those around us, especially the people who society snubs or overlooks. Or even if we recognize others' needs, pride often keeps us from ministering to them, like the people who *"rebuked"* a blind man so they could hear and see Jesus in Mark 10:48. They were turning toward Jesus but away from a man He wanted to help and heal — which meant *they* were the ones who were truly blind.

Greed, self-importance, and pride are roadblocks to servanthood. Jesus challenges His followers to put themselves last.

What does this mean for us? It may mean taking the least desirable task at work or home, spending time with a lonely person, bringing a meal to someone, covering costs in a crisis, serving without being seen, fostering a child, or doing mission work in a hard place. However we live out servanthood, we model our Savior, Jesus Christ, and give others a glimpse of His heart.

PRAYER

Heavenly Father, change my heart to care less about money or praise and care more about people. Help me see people like You see them, soften my heart to their struggles, and give me a real desire to minister to their needs. Help me count others more significant than myself. Remove the roadblocks that stand in my way — I want to follow You fully and completely. In Jesus' name, amen.

NOTES

NOTES

WEEK SIX

DAY 26

MARK 12:1-27

Jesus told the parable of the tenants and answered difficult questions.

As we kick off our sixth week of Bible study, today's reading also begins a new chapter of Mark. But did you know chapter divisions are actually not original to the biblical text? They were added by a Bible scholar in the 13th century to make it easier for people to navigate and reference the Scriptures, but this occurred almost 1,200 years *after* Mark wrote his Gospel. So to identify the "*them*" to whom Jesus spoke in Mark 12:1, we have to flip back to the end of Chapter 11.

To whom was Jesus speaking in Mark 11:27-33? Who, then, was the audience of Jesus' parables in Mark 12:1?

Now read Mark 12:1-11, and briefly summarize the parable of the tenants:

Jesus' previous parables had concealed God's Truth from hard-hearted people (Mark 4:11-12), but this parable revealed Truth to them. When Jesus told the parable of the tenants, the hard-hearted scribes and Pharisees likely recognized the vineyard as a symbol of God's relationship to Israel based on Old Testament verses like Isaiah 5:1-7. They likely thought, at least at first, that the landowner in the parable represented them, the Jewish people, and the tenants symbolized the Romans. But as Jesus' story unfolds, it becomes clear that *God* is the landowner and *His own people* were like evil tenants who would reject and kill His servants (prophets) and His Son (Jesus).[1] This parable didn't bode well for its hearers, as it concludes with the tenants' destruction.

Like the tenants of the parable, what did the men listening to Jesus want to do to Him, according to Mark 12:12? Why had they not yet done so?

Attempting to undermine His authority with the crowd, Pharisees and Herodians came to try to trap Jesus with a political question: *"Is it lawful to pay taxes to Caesar, or not?"* (Mark 12:14). If Jesus answered "yes," He would alienate Jewish people in the crowd who resented their Roman oppressors. But if Jesus answered "no," the religious leaders could arrest Him and turn him over to Roman authorities to be executed for sedition and treason, or betraying the Roman Empire.[2]

Jesus answered by shifting the conversation to a matter far more important than money and taxes: the matter of **image** and **identity**. He first pointed out that Roman coins bore Caesar's image, so they *"are Caesar's"* (Mark 12:17).

What does this mean about us as human beings since we bear *God's* image (Genesis 1:27)? Who do we belong to, and how does that shape our lives and loyalties?

Next, the Sadducees, members of a religious sect of Judaism, came to Jesus and asked a question about resurrection — in which they did not believe (Mark 12:18).

Read Mark 12:19-23. What did the Sadducees ask Jesus? How does this absurd and complicated hypothetical scenario show that they were trying *"to trap him"* (v. 13)?

Rather than answering their question, Jesus again addressed the more important issue at hand: their denial of the resurrection. The doctrine of resurrection is clearly set out in Daniel 12:1-2 and alluded to in other Old Testament passages like Job 19:26, Psalm 16:9-11, Isaiah 25:7-8, Isaiah 26:19, and Hosea 13:14; however, the Sadducees only accepted the Torah (Genesis-Deuteronomy) as inspired Scripture.[3] So Jesus corrected their error.

Jesus even pointed out that Exodus 3 — a passage found in the Torah — alludes to *"the dead being raised"* in the very nature of God's abiding covenant (Mark 12:26). Jesus also affirmed that believers in eternity will be "*like angels in heaven,*" though Sadducees also did not believe in angels ... so they were *"quite wrong"* in multiple ways (vv. 25-27).[4]

While the Sadducees denied that there will be a resurrection of the dead, why is the resurrection of Jesus and the hope of our own resurrection essential to our faith? How might you explain this if someone questioned you about it today? (See 1 Corinthians 15:12-58.)

WHAT IS THE SANHEDRIN?

Many of the chief priests, scribes, and elders to whom Jesus spoke were members of the Sanhedrin, the governing body that constituted the highest Jewish authority in Israel during Jesus' time. It was composed of 70 members and presided over by the high priest, who acted as the final authority on matters of Old Testament law.[5] *Because of the Sanhedrin's position of leadership and influence, members would eventually sway public opinion against Jesus (as we'll see later in Mark 15), setting the stage for His crucifixion.*

DAY 27

MARK 12:28-44

Jesus taught more, affirmed the greatest commandment, and praised a widow's offering.

Who? What? When? Where? Why? These are sometimes known as "journalistic questions." By this point in Mark's narrative, Jesus had experienced a barrage of questions from the Sanhedrin (Mark 11:27-33), the Pharisees and Herodians (Mark 12:13-17), and the Sadducees (Mark 12:18-27). In today's reading, one last person approached Jesus in the temple and asked a question.

In Mark 12:28, what did the scribe ask? Does his question, and his motivation for asking it, seem the same or different from other questioners we've seen so far?

Famous rabbis were often asked this question, as there were 613 commands in the Law of Moses.[1] While some laws were considered smaller and some greater, they were *all* to be obeyed, so this wasn't an inquiry about which laws could be ignored. It was about the *fundamental idea* on which all 613 commands rest.[2]

Jesus answered in Mark 12:29-31 by quoting the first part of the *Shema*, a confession of faith recorded in Deuteronomy 6:4-9 that pious Jews recited in the morning and evening each day. The *Shema* is a declaration of God's oneness and a reminder to love Him with heart, soul, and strength. Jesus added "*with all your mind*" in Mark 12:30 and attached a second command also found in the Old Testament: *"Love your neighbor as yourself"* (Leviticus 19:18).

In Mark 12:32-34, the man accepted Jesus' answer and went on to say that loving God and neighbor is *"much more than"* what? Why do you think Jesus considered this a wise response?

When Jesus overturned the tables in the temple in Mark 11:15-17, He prophetically overturned temple sacrifices as worship. Soon there would be no need for burnt offerings and sacrifices because Jesus Himself would serve as the *ultimate sacrifice* for sin. The scribe's words in today's reading reinforced what Jesus had already begun to demonstrate: Love for God and neighbor is the heart of well-pleasing worship.[3] And Jesus would model *perfect love* on the cross.

After answering questions, Jesus posed a question of His own in Mark 12:35-37 that hinted at His identity and purpose: If *"the Christ is the son of David,"* as the scribes said, how could the Messiah also be David's "*Lord*"? Jesus did not answer His own question but instead allowed the audience to work out for themselves that the Messiah is more than just David's descendant. He is also David's superior, and His Kingdom is far greater than David's kingdom.[4]

> Having addressed the scribes' beliefs, Jesus turned His attention to their behaviors in verses 38-40. What practices or behaviors did Jesus criticize, and why?

Essentially, if we think back to the fig tree from Mark 11, the scribes were all "leaves" and no "fruit." They appeared to love God, but they were hypocrites — pretenders. Really, they loved their high social status and position. Instead of the Kingdom of God, they loved the kingdom they had made for themselves.

In stark contrast, a widow of low status entered the temple in Mark 12:42. This would have been in the "Court of the Women," which was the location of "*the treasury*" and "*offering box*" noted in verse 41. In 13 Shofar-chests (trumpet-shaped receptacles), worshippers placed their monetary offerings. While rich people were giving large sums, the widow threw in only two copper coins, or *lepton* in Greek, which means "a tiny thing." This was the smallest coin in circulation in Israel.[5]

Onlookers would have noticed the many coins of the rich, which may have even created loud noises as they clinked and clanged against the receptacles. But who would take notice of a widow and her two tiny coins? *Jesus did.*

> What did Jesus say of the widow's offering in verses 43-44? How might these words of approval for a sacrificial gift relate to His own upcoming sacrifice on the cross?

Like bookends framing this segment of Jesus' ministry, His time in the temple began with the *condemnation* of buyers and sellers and ended with the *commendation* of a widow.[6] While the buyers and sellers turned the temple into a place of economic gain, the widow faithfully gave what little she had for the temple's sake. She placed God's Kingdom above her own.

How are you putting God's Kingdom above your own — seeking God's will, serving sacrificially, engaging in spiritual growth, and pointing people to Jesus? What's one practical way you can love God and love others today?

MAP OF THE TEMPLE

IN JESUS' DAY

The view on the left shows the temple's general position and surrounding areas. The view on the right shows close-up details of the temple layout and inner courts.

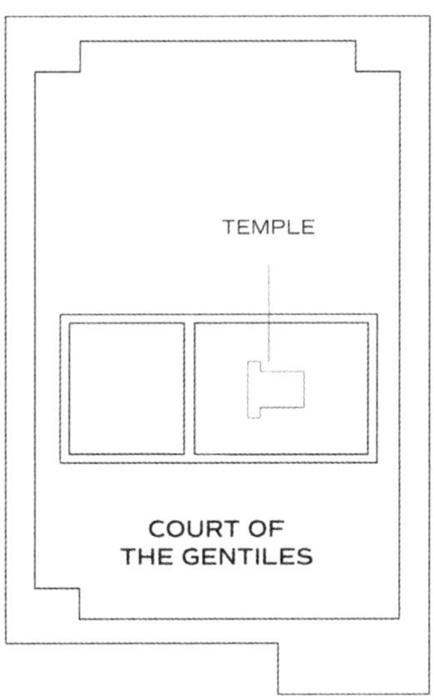

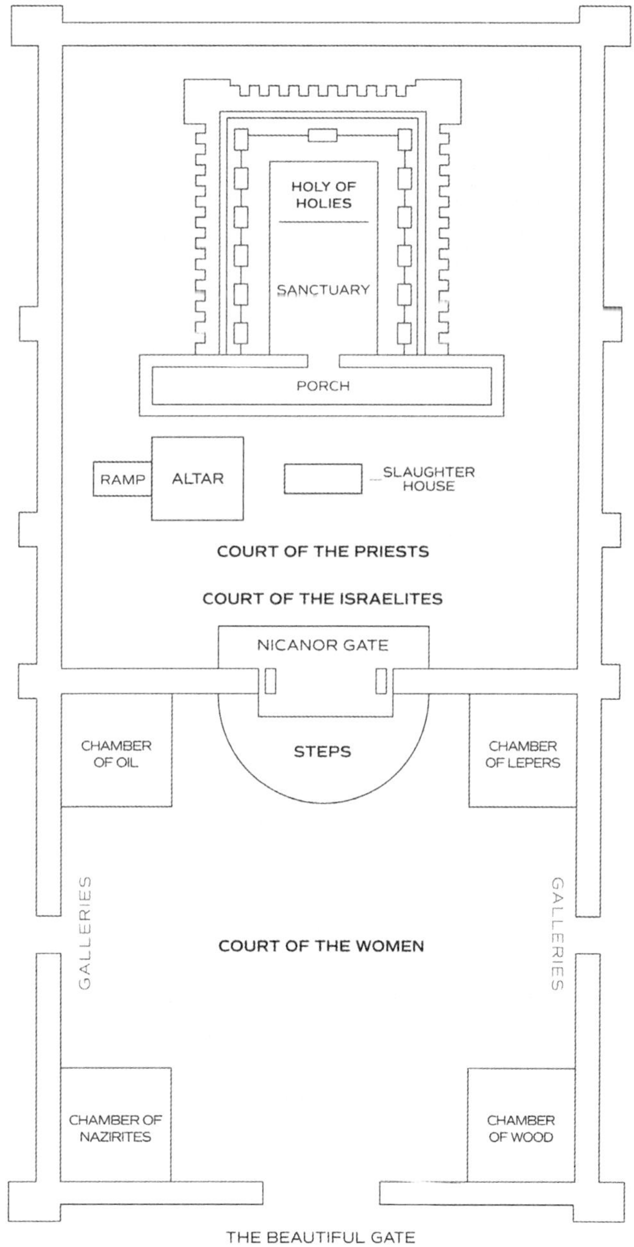

Adapted from: Byfield, Ted. *The Veil Is Torn (The Christians: Their First Two Thousand Years, Volume 1).* The Christian History Project, 2003, p. 46.

DAY 28

MARK 13:1-13

Jesus predicted the destruction of the temple and warned of coming persecution.

Have you ever heard someone say wars and earthquakes are signs the end of the world is near? If so, perhaps without even knowing it, they were quoting the Olivet Discourse, a conversation in which Jesus taught His disciples about the future and end times. This discourse starts in Mark 13:3.

But first, in Mark 13:1-2, Jesus left the temple for the last time. While He was leaving, what did one of His disciples do, and how did He respond?

This temple with its *"wonderful buildings"* (v. 1) was actually the second Jewish temple. The first, built by King Solomon, was destroyed by the Babylonians in 586 B.C., and a second, less impressive temple was constructed around 515 B.C.

In 20 B.C., Herod the Great began replacing, expanding, and renovating the temple and its surrounding structures.[1] This reconstructed temple complex, encompassing 35 acres, was truly a wonder to behold — one of the greatest in the ancient world. The gold-plated exterior of the temple would have gleamed in the sun, and the brilliant white stone facade gave the structure the appearance of a snow-covered mountain.[2]

Yet in Mark 13:2, Jesus foretold what would happen to these great buildings and stones. According to John 2:20-22, how did the future of the temple also relate to Jesus' own future?

Jesus had hinted at God's judgment upon Israel when He cursed the fig tree, cleansed the temple, and told the parable of the tenants in Mark 11-12, and now He plainly told His disciples the temple would be destroyed. Although many Jews of this time thought the temple was invincible, Jesus' words would prove true 40 years later. In A.D. 70, the Roman army reduced the temple to rubble.[3]

For now, Peter, James, John, and Andrew approached Jesus privately on the Mount of Olives in Mark 13:3-4, wanting to know when this would happen and what signs to expect beforehand. Jesus answered by naming things that reveal the ongoing, gradual decline of creation as sin increasingly corrupts the world, saying they *"must take place, but the end is not yet"* (v. 7).

> According to Mark 13:6-8, what are "*the beginning of the birth pains*" (or we might say "the beginning of the end")?

Since the first sin in Genesis 3, humans have been living between two paradises — the first creation and the new creation to come (Isaiah 65:17; Revelation 21:1-5). In the meantime, while we wait for the ultimate restoration of all things, we reside in a fallen world where sin, suffering, war, and natural disasters are an ever-present reality.

> In Mark 13:9-13, what else did Jesus tell His disciples to anticipate? How did He promise to help them through it?

Earlier, Jesus said to a crowd that anyone who wants to follow Him must *"take up his cross"* (Mark 8:34), and again here, Jesus warned that following Him comes with a cost. His followers would be persecuted by both Jews and gentiles. But despite the persecution, the gospel would endure and "*be proclaimed to all nations*" (Mark 13:10).

While we don't necessarily see this happen in Mark's Gospel, we can look to other scriptures, like the book of Acts, to see the first recorded gentile conversions to Christianity. And Paul's letters in the New Testament not only mention gentile converts but are the oldest surviving Christian writings we have, giving us a firsthand look at how gentiles were already being folded into the Church even within 20 years of Jesus' resurrection! The dissemination of the gospel in Rome is further recorded in Acts 28; by the time the temple was destroyed, just as Jesus foretold, the Good News would already reach the edges of the Roman Empire.[4]

Let's look again at Mark 13:13. The ones who endure persecution for the sake of Christ *"will be"* what? Alongside 2 Timothy 2:12, Romans 8:17, and James 1:12, how does this inspire you to stay faithful and hold to the Truth?

DAY 29

MARK 13:14-37

Jesus foretold of tribulation before His return and urged watchfulness.

Buckle up, friends! Today's passage continues Jesus' Olivet Discourse and His teachings about things to come — and some of them are tough with a capital "T." But this passage is worth wrestling with because it points us straight to eternal hope. Are you ready?

Let's rejoin the conversation as four of Jesus' disciples asked when they should expect the temple's destruction. Rather than providing a specific date, Jesus foretold of an event that would serve as their sign.

In Mark 13:14, what did Jesus say they would see?

The phrase "*abomination of desolation*" (v. 14), which has been the subject of much debate, is also found in the Old Testament book of Daniel. "*Abomination*" in this context means something loathsome or repugnant to God and is often associated with pagan worship (Deuteronomy 18:11-12; Proverbs 6:16).[1] This term, coupled with "*desolation*," suggests sacrilege that causes the ruin or desecration of a holy place.[2]

What was prophesied in Daniel 11:31? How might this help us understand Mark 13:14?

In 167 B.C., nearly four centuries after Daniel's prophecy, the pagan ruler Antiochus IV desecrated the Jewish temple by erecting a statue of the Greek god Zeus inside and sacrificing a pig (an animal God declared unclean in Leviticus 11:7) on the altar.[3] Generations later, Jesus may have been warning of another similar desecration of the temple to come.

Some suggest Jesus' words in Mark 13:14 predicted events around 67-68 A.D., when John of Gischala led the Zealots (Jewish revolutionaries) into the temple, made it their headquarters, and appointed their own high priest.[4] While the Zealots were in control, criminals entered the holiest places and even committed murder inside the temple.[5] According to historical documents from this time, the high priest Ananus lamented that God's house was "laden with such abominations," and its sacred chambers were "crowded with the feet of murderers."[6]

Beyond these fulfillments of Daniel and Jesus' prophecies, some scholars suggest these passages also anticipate a future *"abomination of desolation"* that will precede Christ's return at the end of the age.[7] The Greek word for "*abomination*" is used six times in the Bible, and three are in the book of Revelation, which often refers to the return of Jesus (Revelation 17:4-5, Revelation 21:27).

> In Mark 13:14-16, what did Jesus instruct the people of Judea to do when they recognized the sign? How might this urgency also apply to the future return of Jesus and His judgment of the world?

Jesus warned that the tribulation in Jerusalem would be unprecedented. And if we interpret this prophecy in the context of A.D. 70, we know *it was*. According to the first-century historian Josephus, outside the city walls, Jews were crucified in such large numbers that the Romans ran out of wood for crosses. Inside the city, Jews endured fighting, murder, famine, disease, and even cannibalism. When Rome laid siege to the city, up to 1,100,000 Jews were killed and 97,000 taken captive.[8] Though Josephus' numbers are thought to be exaggerated, they underscore the innumerable casualties.

Some scholars interpret Mark 13:19-23 as a description of these events in A.D. 70, and others interpret the same verses as a reference to a great end-time tribulation for believers. Either way, in verses 24-27, Jesus clearly shifted to speak about His future return *"coming in clouds with great power"* to gather His people to Himself.

> How does this image of an all-powerful, redeeming Jesus provide comfort and hope despite any confusion or fear stirred by the other prophecies in Mark 13?

Finally, Jesus concluded the Olivet Discourse with two parables. The first, which Jesus applied directly to *"this generation"* of His listeners (Mark 13:30), seems to relate to the destruction of Jerusalem. The second parable seems to relate to His return at the end of the age.[9]

Read Mark 13:32-37. What lesson does this parable teach us?

Jesus concluded with a command to *"stay awake"* (v. 37). What does it mean to be a "sleeping" Christian? What does it mean to be "awake," and how can we make sure we stay that way?

DAY 30

MARK 14:1-31

Jesus was anointed, predicted that He would be betrayed, and shared the Last Supper.

Compared to the other Gospels, reading Mark's fast-paced account sometimes feels like watching a video at one-and-a-half times the normal speed. You may have noticed the author's frequent use of the word "*immediately*" (more than 30 times throughout the Gospel!), which rapidly propels the story forward.

Following this pattern, the final two chapters are a whirlwind of events. Mark 14 begins just as Jerusalem's Passover festivities were commencing — and from here, we'll see the plot to kill Jesus progress at a breakneck pace.

Based on Exodus 12:24-27, what did the Passover celebration mean to the Jewish people?

In Mark 14, somewhere between 85,000 and 300,000 pilgrims had traveled to Jerusalem for the Passover festival, and both Jewish and Roman authorities were on high alert. Disturbances and riots were a real possibility because a celebration of Israel's past liberation from Egyptian rule could easily stir up the people's hopes of an upcoming liberation, this time from Roman rule.[1]

Fearing the crowds, the chief priests were hesitant to kill Jesus during the feast, yet they still made arrangements to kill Him soon. Mark 14:10 tells us Judas Iscariot agreed to hand Jesus over to the chief priests in exchange for money (30 pieces of silver, according to Matthew 26:15). If these coins were shekels worth four denarii each, the payment amounted to about 120 days' wages.[2]

Such a betrayal begs the question: What is Jesus worth? To Judas, He was worth 30 coins. Yet to an unnamed woman in the house of Simon the leper, Jesus was worth her most precious and costly possession.

What did this woman do in Mark 14:3-9, and what did Jesus say about her actions? How does this compare to the actions of the widow in Mark 12:41-44?

Mark doesn't give us the reason behind the woman's actions, but we know her alabaster flask and its contents were worth about a year's wages and may have even been a family heirloom.[3] We also know anointing, or pouring oil on someone as a sign of honor, was common at feasts, so perhaps she was extending a common courtesy, though in a most uncommon and extravagant way.[4] Maybe she wanted to show gratitude for a miracle Jesus had performed. Maybe she recognized Jesus as the Messiah and anointed Him to declare His kingship, as had happened with some past Israelite kings (1 Samuel 10:1; 2 Kings 9:1-6).[5]

But Jesus wasn't only the King of Israel who would crush the nation's enemies; He was the King who would crush Satan and liberate people from the bondage of sin. Rather than immediately sit on an earthly throne, He would hang on a cross. And if there were still any misconceptions about this, Jesus cleared them up by declaring, *"She has anointed my body beforehand for burial"* (Mark 14:8). Some scholars believe this woman was the only person in the room who understood Jesus' teaching well enough to recognize His imminent death and burial.[6]

Next, in Mark 14:16-25, Jesus and the 12 gathered in an upper room to share the Passover meal, and He taught them more about the meaning of His self-sacrifice.

In your own words, summarize the events that took place at the Last Supper. Even if you've read this passage before, what stands out to you?

On this night, Jesus made a new covenant with His body and blood. The Old Testament law required priests to kill animals and pour their blood on the altar to atone for sins. But Jesus was about to become a new sacrifice to God that would eliminate the need for any future sacrifices.[7]

What does Hebrews 10:1-4 say about animal sacrifices? How does this compare to Jesus' sacrifice (Hebrews 10:10-12)?

In Mark 14:29-31, what did Peter promise (similar to James and John's promise in Mark 10:38-39)? How do these fickle human promises compare to the promises Jesus Himself made in today's passage?

Even as He broke bread with His friends around the table, Jesus knew Judas would betray Him, Peter would deny Him, and all of His disciples would fall away. Yet despite the inevitable failure of sinful people who *"fall short of the glory of God"* (Romans 3:23) — including us, too — Jesus' love never wavered. He would walk the lonely road to the cross so our sins could be forgiven.

THE LORD'S SUPPER:

FOUR CUPS AND A FUTURE CELEBRATION

Jews ate the Passover meal every year at nightfall on the 14th day of the month of Nissan, which corresponds with March 27-April 25 on modern calendars. A lamb was killed and prepared beforehand, to be eaten with unleavened bread and bitter herbs, which symbolized the bitterness of Israel's slavery in Egypt. The meal was to be eaten while reclining, which was a symbol of freedom.[1]

By the first century, Jewish custom also included **four cups of wine** during the Passover meal, each connected to the promises of Exodus 6:6-7. At this time in history, these were often diluted with water, according to Greco-Roman drinking practices and Jewish rabbinic sources.

1. **The first cup**, the *Kiddush* cup, would begin the celebration, followed by eating the bitter herbs.[2]

2. Over **the second cup**, Israelites would tell the story of their exodus from Egypt and sing Psalms 113-114.[3] After the second cup, the full meal would begin with a blessing of the unleavened bread, eaten with the roasted lamb.[4] Customarily, the blessing was: "This is the bread of affliction our ancestors ate when they came from Egypt."[5] However, Jesus departed from tradition and gave the bread a new meaning in Mark 14:22, saying, "*Take; this is my body.*"

3. When it was time to take the next cup, Jesus said, "*This is my blood of the covenant, which is poured out for many*" (Mark 14:24). Assuming this was **the third cup** of the Passover meal, it was linked to God's promise in Exodus 6:6: "*I will redeem you with an outstretched arm.*"[6] God's arm had overpowered the Egyptian Pharaoh and liberated the Israelites from slavery. And now Jesus gave this, too, a new meaning — His outstretched arms on the cross would overpower sin, and His redeeming blood would liberate us from sin's shackles. Just as blood sealed God's covenant in Exodus 24:8, Jesus' death on the cross would ratify the new covenant.[7]

4. Based on Mark 14:25, some scholars assume Jesus abstained from drinking **the fourth cup**, the *Hallel* cup or "cup of praise." This final cup was traditionally linked to the phrase "*I will take you to be my people*" in Exodus 6:7, which is the ultimate goal of God's redemptive plan. Jesus announced, *"I will not drink again of the fruit of the vine until that day when I drink it new in the kingdom of God"* (Mark 14:25), alluding to a heavenly banquet. This idea is woven through Scripture, including the prophet Isaiah's description of a future feast where there will be no more death and tears (Isaiah 25:6-8).

In Revelation 19:6-9, the Apostle John's words also illustrate a future marriage supper celebrating the eternal union between believers and Jesus Christ. As Jesus ate His final meal with the disciples, He was well aware of the ordeal that lay ahead, yet He concluded with His eyes fixed on this joyous celebration still to come.

WEEK 6

WEEKEND REFLECTION

& PRAYER

WHAT'S BEHIND THE LEAVES

Have you ever opened a bag of potato chips only to realize it was mostly filled with air? The bag appears deceptively large — until it's opened and its sparse contents are exposed. In this week's reading, Jesus encountered three things that were deceptive in appearance:

1. A leafy fig tree that appeared fruitful but was not (Mark 11:12-14).
2. An impressive temple that appeared to be a house of worship but had become a place of corruption and hypocrisy (Mark 11:15-17).
3. Religious leaders who appeared holy and devout but prioritized power and position (Mark 12:1-12).

No deception goes unseen by God. At the very beginning, in Genesis 3:7-8, Adam and Eve sinned and tried to cover themselves with fig leaves and hide among the trees in Eden. But God knew what they had done. In our own lives, we can also try to feign righteousness and put on a show for all to see, but even if we successfully fool others, we can never fool God. He knows what's behind the pretense. He sees behind the leaves — and He wants us to bear good fruit.

Best of all, God Himself is the source of true spiritual growth. Apart from Him, we will never be a *"healthy tree"* that bears good fruit (Matthew 7:17-18). But if we belong to Jesus Christ, we can be *"filled with the fruit of righteousness"* as Jesus breaks the power of our passions and the harmful desires of our flesh (Philippians 1:11). When we live by the Holy Spirit and He lives in us, we bear fruit of *"love, joy, peace, patience, kindness, goodness, faithfulness, gentleness, [and] self-control"* (Galatians 5:22-23).

PRAYER

Heavenly Father, please forgive me for my sins and shortcomings. I know You see them all. Create in me a clean heart, and help me to choose righteousness in all situations. I don't want to be like a fruitless Pharisee. Empower me with Your Spirit so I might be more loving, joyful, peaceful, patient, kind, good, faithful, and self-controlled. In Jesus' name, amen.

NOTES

NOTES

WEEK SEVEN

DAY 31

MARK 14:32-52

Jesus prayed in Gethsemane and was arrested by a crowd led by Judas.

Is there any greater emotional sting than betrayal and abandonment by the people you love? Jesus knows what that feels like. In today's reading, just as Jesus foretold, one of the 12 betrayed Him and the rest abandoned Him.

After the Passover meal, Jesus went to the garden of Gethsemane with 11 disciples (Judas had already left to betray Him), and then He went even deeper into the garden with His three closest disciples. These were the same three who had stood with Jesus on the glorious Mount of Transfiguration in Mark 9.

How do you think Peter, James, and John felt now, called to pray with Jesus in the dark of night while He was "*greatly distressed and troubled*" (Mark 14:33)? How do *you* feel as you behold Jesus both on the mountaintop of power and in the garden of suffering?

Jesus' distress in Gethsemane was not that of a person whose plans had gone awry but that of a master in full control, aware of the trials ahead. Neither arrest, abuse, interrogations, beatings, nor crucifixion would take Jesus by surprise — yet even with such foreknowledge, His soul was grieved.[1]

In Mark 14:35, Jesus walked a little farther to be alone. What did He do before He began to pray? Also read Matthew 26:39.

When we think of Jesus praying, we might imagine Him kneeling with His hands calmly clasped (like in Heinrich Hofmann's famous painting *Christ in Gethsemane*). But how does this compare to the Gospel accounts of Jesus' posture in the garden? Why is it important for us to correctly envision Jesus as He truly was in this moment?

Jews typically prayed in a standing position with their hands lifted, but in times of extreme urgency, they would lie flat on the ground in prostration (e.g., Deuteronomy 9:18).[2] One Bible commentator notes that Jesus' position here could be a sign of sorrow, submission to His Father, or both.[3]

What did Jesus ask the Father to do in Mark 14:36? How does this prayer reveal and remind us of Jesus' humanity?

Jesus' divinity has been on full display throughout the Gospel of Mark as He taught with authority and demonstrated power over demons, nature, sickness, and sin; however, we've also seen His humanity, perhaps most clearly in moments when Jesus was tired (Mark 4:38), hungry (Mark 11:12), or disappointed (Mark 8:17; Mark 8:21).[4] Jesus' humanity is just as important as His divinity because only a perfect *human* could pay the penalty for *humanity*'s sins. Because the Father did not "*remove this cup*" and eliminate the cross (Mark 14:36), it is clear that Jesus' death truly was the only way for humankind to be saved.[5]

Jesus finished His prayer in verse 36 by saying, "*Yet not what I will, but what you will.*" What does this mean, and how does it serve as a model prayer for us today?

In Mark 14:38-40, what instructions about prayer did Jesus give to Peter, James, and John? What did they do instead? What does it tell us about Jesus that He would lose His life for disciples who wouldn't even lose sleep for Him?

In today's final scriptures, Jesus reprimanded His disciples and announced His betrayer was close. When Judas and a band of armed men arrived, one disciple reacted with violence, but Jesus quickly put an end to it. He knew He must go with the men for Scripture to be fulfilled and God's salvific plan to be carried out.

At the moment of Jesus' arrest, His disciples fled, just as He knew they would. Many more prophecies would be fulfilled in the hours that followed, and already the words of Zechariah rang true: "*Strike the shepherd, and the sheep will be scattered ...*" (Zechariah 13:7).

DAY 32

MARK 14:53-72

Jesus was tried before the Jewish council while Peter denied Him three times.

Have you ever tried to watch two screens at the same time, each playing a different show or sporting event? It's not easy to give equal attention to two things that are happening at once, but that's what we will do as we read today's passage. The latter verses of Mark 14 record two simultaneous events: Jesus' trial and Peter's denial.

After His arrest, Jesus was brought before the Sanhedrin, a council of chief priests, scribes, and elders presided over by the high priest, Caiaphas. But the proceedings recorded in Mark 14 departed from proper legal procedure. Trials were not supposed to be held in the palace of the high priest, nor at night, nor on the eve of a feast day; however, Jesus was tried *"right [in] the courtyard of the high priest"* in the middle of the night during Passover (v. 54). Furthermore, a verdict for a capital offense should have taken two days of proceedings, but Jesus was issued a same-day conviction.[1]

While these laws were perhaps more strictly enforced after the time of Jesus, the violations still suggest some aspects of Jesus' trial were illegal. It is possible the Sanhedrin cited Deuteronomy 17:13 as a loophole, claiming Jesus' offense was so serious that He had to be tried and condemned *immediately* so His case would serve as a deterrent to all who "*hear and fear.*"[2]

Deuteronomy 17:6 required at least two witnesses to give evidence in capital cases. According to Mark 14:55-59, why was this a challenge at Jesus' trial?

Compare Isaiah 53:7 to Mark 14:61. How did Jesus fulfill this prophecy of the suffering Servant?

Caiaphas interrogated Jesus by asking if He was *"the Son of the Blessed"* in Mark 14:61, meaning the Son of God. Jews substituted "God" with other reverent names (like "the Blessed") to avoid taking the Lord's name in vain. In this case, the high priest was so blind to his own hypocrisy that he was about to condemn God Himself to death — using "reverent" language as he did.

Jews expected the Messiah to have a Father-Son relationship with God based on His promise to King David's descendants in 2 Samuel 7:14-15.[3] But when Caiaphas asked whether Jesus was the Son of God, he wasn't genuinely asking whether Jesus was divine. He was asking whether Jesus *claimed* to be the Messiah because he wanted to accuse Jesus of blasphemy.

How did Jesus answer the high priest in Mark 14:62?

When He answered, Jesus not only publicly revealed His identity as the Messiah but His position "*at the right hand of Power*" (v. 62). He also returned and reversed Caiaphas' so-called reverence here by using "*Power*" as a substitute for "God."

Read Mark 14:63-65. How did the following people respond to Jesus' claims?

- High priest: ______________________________
- Members of the Sanhedrin: ______________________________
- Guards: ______________________________

We see even more tragic irony in the taunt to "*prophesy*" (v. 65) — because that *very night*, three things had already happened as Jesus foretold. First, He was betrayed to the chief priests and teachers who condemned Him to death and were turning Him over the gentiles (as prophesied in Mark 10:33). Second, His disciples were scattered (as prophesied in Mark 14:27). And third, Peter denied Him (as prophesied in Mark 14:30).[4]

Hours earlier, Peter had expressed his willingness to follow Jesus anywhere. He was the only disciple to follow Jesus to the high priest's home ... but he did so from a safe distance. And when he was recognized as Jesus' follower, he vehemently denied knowing Jesus again and again. He even "*began to invoke a curse on himself*" in his final denial (Mark 14:71), which was like saying, "If I'm not telling the truth right now, may God strike me dead."

Look back at the parable of the sower in Mark 4:13-20. Peter's actions are similar to which seed in Jesus' parable?

Peter crumbled under the threat of arrest. But this momentary failure would not disqualify him from someday becoming a devoted apostle. Even though his faith was rocky on the night of Jesus' arrest, Jesus would later say of him, *"On this rock I will build my church"* (Matthew 16:18). Peter faltered — as we do, too — but as we've seen throughout our study of Mark, Jesus is the Savior who never lets us go.

DAY 33

MARK 15:1-32

Jesus was condemned by Pilate, mocked, and crucified alongside criminals.

Think of the last time you had a *really long* night. Through hours of darkness, every sleepless second feels agonizing ...

As night became morning after Jesus' arrest, the Sanhedrin charged Him with blasphemy, but they did not have the authority to carry out capital punishment because they were under the rule of Caesar. So they transferred Jesus to the Roman governor, Pontius Pilate.[1]

Many first-century historians describe Pilate as cruel and insensitive to Jewish faith and practice.[2] A charge of blasphemy hardly would have concerned a pagan governor with no regard for Jewish beliefs. But in Mark 15:2, Pilate asked Jesus a political question, not a religious one: *"Are you the King of the Jews?"* Mark didn't specifically say so, but Pilate's question suggests the religious leaders had accused Jesus of sedition against Rome and claiming royal authority.[3]

These were false charges. Jesus is the prophesied messianic King — but not in the context they accused. He never incited rebellion nor had imperial ambitions. In fact, Jesus rebuked and corrected disciples who expressed militaristic or political expectations (Mark 8:31-33; Mark 10:35-45). Though one day Jesus will return with *"the armies of heaven"* (Revelation 19:14) and establish His Kingdom on earth in its fullness, His is not merely an earthly kingdom with physical borders, political systems, and military pursuits.

This is very different from how Pilate managed his "kingdom," which involved strategic concessions and political favors. According to Mark 15:6, what did Pilate do for the Jews during the Passover feast?

Although Jesus seemed to be the obvious choice for release, the chief priests stirred up the crowd to choose Barabbas, an *actual* insurrectionist. Jesus, who was innocent and never incited rebellion against Rome, would hang on a cross while the guilty rebel walked free.

How does this idea of substitution (Jesus in Barabbas' place) deepen your understanding of God's grace toward sinners? Toward you?

Before Jesus died on the cross that was meant for Barabbas, what happened to Him in Mark 15:16-20? How does this match what was written long before in Isaiah 53:3?

Mark 15:15 briefly mentions that Jesus was "*scourged*." This punishment was customarily carried out prior to a crucifixion, but sometimes scourging proved fatal itself. Prisoners were bound to a post and lashed with a whip barbed with bits of bone, lead, or bronze on the ends of leather cords, designed to rip off the flesh.[4] A particularly brutal scourging may be the reason Jesus did not carry His own cross to the execution site. Instead, a man named Simon carried Jesus' cross to Golgotha.

Interestingly, Mark 15:21 notes that Simon was "*the father of Alexander and Rufus,*" and in Paul's letter to the first-century Roman church, he said, "*Greet Rufus, chosen in the Lord*" (Romans 16:13). If these are the same Rufus, it means Simon's son grew up to become a prominent church leader and follower of Jesus. How does this showcase God's redemptive work?

Crucifixion was a horrific means of execution that served two purposes in the Roman Empire:

1. It was a lengthy punishment that prolonged pain sometimes for days as the victim, an enemy of Rome, slowly died from asphyxiation. This was meant to display Rome's power.

2. It was a public spectacle. The victim usually carried the cross to which he would be nailed, then was crucified with a placard announcing his crime, which served as a deterrent to other criminals in the populace.[5] Adding to the brutality of the cross, while hanging to die, victims were often subjected to public contempt and verbal abuse.[6]

In Mark 15:29-32, who mocked and insulted Jesus while He hung on the cross?

Who was crucified at Jesus' right and left in Mark 15:27? Now look back at Mark 10:35-40. Did James and John understand what they were asking?

"Come down now from the cross that we may see and believe" (Mark 15:32) was the ultimate ironic mockery of Jesus. Because it is the very act of *staying on the cross* that fulfilled His messianic purpose to bring salvation to humanity. He stayed on the cross so the Kingdom of God would be accessible to sinners like us.

DAY 34

MARK 15:33-47

Jesus died, the temple curtain tore, and He was buried in a tomb.

It seems fitting that on the spiritually darkest day in history, the land was also literally covered in darkness. After Jesus had been on the cross for three hours, darkness fell and lingered from noon until 3 p.m. (Note that Mark 15:33 says *"the sixth hour ... until the ninth hour,"* but this is because Jews considered sunrise to be the first hour of the day.)

Darkness often symbolizes mourning or marks the death of significant individuals. In this instance, *"darkness over the whole land"* (v. 33) also may have been a sign of God's judgment, particularly reminiscent of the ninth plague against Egypt in Exodus 10:21-23.[1]

Why would it be significant for Jesus' crucifixion to echo or connect to previous events in the history of God's people, like the exodus from Egypt?

After Jesus had been on the cross for six hours, He cried out. What did He say in Mark 15:34? Now read Psalm 22:1. Why do you think Jesus spoke these words?

Long ago, the psalmist David began his prayer with a lament of abandonment ... but he eventually came to the realization that God had "*not hidden his face from him*" (Psalm 22:24). God heard David's cries. And his prayer concluded with vindication and restoration.

If Jesus had the whole of Psalm 22 in mind when He was on the cross, then His cry was not just one of despair but one of assured victory.[2] Still, in this moment, Mark says He did not cry out the latter words of assurance but only the opening lament. Jesus cried out under the full weight of God's judgment as He bore the sins of the world "*by becoming a curse for us*" (Galatians 3:13).[3]

Like many people throughout His life, the crowds in Mark 15:35-36 also misunderstood Jesus at His death. What did they think He said, and what did someone do?

At a glance, this incident may read like a mocking and cruel gesture toward the dying Jesus. Luke 23:36 records an event in which soldiers cruelly offered sour wine to prolong Jesus' suffering. But while one of those soldiers could be the "*someone*" in Mark 15:36, it is possible Mark recorded a different event entirely.

Elijah was believed to be the rescuer of righteous Jews, and some bystanders may have believed Elijah would come to save Jesus. Perhaps the anonymous person who offered Him a drink was a Jew with good intentions to prolong Jesus' life in hopes of a supernatural rescue.[4] The "*sour wine*" in Mark 15:36 was a common thirst-quencher in Jesus' time, a mixture of water and vinegar or old wine. Called *posca* in the ancient Mediterranean, it was cheap, mildly acidic, and safe to drink, which made it popular among soldiers, laborers, and travelers.[5]

Unlike typical victims of crucifixion, Jesus remained conscious until His final breath. After His death, what other atypical things happened in Mark 15:37-39?

Two curtains hung in the temple: one in front of the Holy Place and one in front of the Holy of Holies (see the temple map on Page 129). Scholars debate which curtain *"was torn in two, from top to bottom"* in Mark 15:38, but the inner curtain is perhaps more theologically significant. It separated God from sinful humanity, so its tearing would represent the end of temple sacrifices for sin and a new way to enter the presence of God through Christ. A torn inner curtain aligns with Hebrews 10:19-20, which tells us believers can "*enter the holy places by the blood of Jesus, by the new and living way that he opened for us through the curtain.*"[6]

Finally, in Mark 15:40-41, who did Mark list as witnesses of Jesus' crucifixion? Who was *not present*? (See Mark 14:50 for a reminder.)

According to Mark 15:42-47 (particularly the final verse), who was also present at Jesus' burial, and what might this tell us about the women who were His disciples? How can we follow their example and act as a faithful remnant, staying by Jesus' side no matter what?

DAY 35

MARK 16

Jesus rose from the dead and commissioned His disciples to proclaim the gospel.

We can only imagine the heartbreak Jesus' family and followers felt on the Sabbath when He lay in the tomb. Mark didn't record any events that took place on what surely must have been the most sorrowful day. Instead, after Jesus' burial in Mark 15:47, Mark skipped ahead to resurrection morning.

In Mark 16:1, who went to Jesus' tomb, and why?

Let's just take a moment to appreciate the devotion expressed by these women. They loved Jesus dearly. They were present at His crucifixion, even though it must have been agonizing to witness, and now they were planning to minister to His corpse, even though it would have deteriorated rapidly after being in the tomb.[1]

The typical Jewish burial process included anointing a body with oil *before* it was entombed, but Jesus' burial was rushed since He died just before Sabbath began, and as we learned on Day 6 of our study, doing work on the Sabbath was a serious offense.[2] John 19:39 records that a man named Nicodemus helped Joseph of Arimathea wrap Jesus' body in myrrh and aloes before His burial, so either the women were unaware of this or wanted to do their own anointing.[3] After the Sabbath ended, the women were able to buy spices (to reduce the stench of decay) and went to honor Jesus' body.[4]

They were not approaching the tomb with hope or expectation. In Mark 16:3, they were task-focused and fretful about how they would move the large stone at the entrance. Then a miracle took them completely by surprise.

According to Mark 16:4-5, what did the women see when they arrived at the tomb?

The book of Mark begins and ends with messengers. First, John the Baptist announced what God *would do* in Mark 1, and now the man in white (identified in Matthew 28:2 as *"an angel of the Lord"*) announced what God *has done*.[5]

In Mark 16:6-7, what did the angel tell the women, and what did he order them to do?

Since Peter denied Jesus three times, we might expect verse 7 to say, *"Tell his disciples **except** Peter."* But what does it actually say? What does this reveal about God's forgiveness and second chances?

It is amazing that God chose women to be the first to **receive the Good News** of Jesus' resurrection. In the Ancient Near East, women were thought to be less reliable witnesses than men, and Jews did not even allow women to give testimony in court. Yet the angel commissioned these three supposedly "ineligible" witnesses to go and tell what they saw and heard at Jesus' tomb.

And when Jesus first revealed Himself after His resurrection, it wasn't first to His male disciples but to Mary Magdalene, who then told others (Mark 16:9; John 20:16; Matthew 28:9-10). It is amazing that God also chose a woman to be the first to **share the Good News** that Jesus Christ is alive.

In Mark 16:15, what did Jesus tell His remaining 11 disciples to do? According to Matthew 28:19-20, 1 Peter 2:9, and Romans 10:14-15, who else is this command meant for?

Mark 16:16 reads, "*Whoever believes and is baptized will be saved, but whoever does not believe will be condemned.*" This verse certainly warns against unbelief — but more than that, it's a joyful proclamation of the hope we have in Jesus. Apart from Jesus, *all* people are condemned (John 3:18). One trespass, the first sin in the garden of Eden, led to sin and condemnation for every human. But for all who believe in Jesus, we can escape condemnation because "*one act of righteousness leads to justification and life for all*" (Romans 5:18).

Mark 16:17-20 concludes by mentioning "*signs*" or miraculous acts that Jesus empowered His apostles to do as they spread the gospel and invited people into His Kingdom. But why is it important to remember that Jesus' *"one act"* (Romans 5:18) is the only one that offers eternal redemption? How does this guide you as you share the gospel in your own life?

WHAT IS
AUTHENTICALLY MARK?

As you read the last chapter of Mark, you may have noticed a notation in your Bible stating something like, "Some of the earliest manuscripts do not include Mark 16:9-20." What does this mean?

The oldest Greek manuscripts we have of the Gospel of Mark end with Mark 16:8, an abrupt and jarring conclusion that seems to cut off the narrative at the empty tomb, before the risen Jesus appeared. Verses 9-20, which scholars refer to as the "long ending" of Mark, are included in later manuscripts but are thought to be a non-Markan addition — meaning Mark himself didn't write them, but later scribes may have added these verses to tell the rest of the true story of Jesus' resurrection, as is also attested in the other three Gospel accounts.

Eusebius (A.D. 260-339) and Jerome (A.D. 347-420), respected leaders and historians in the early Church, both stated that their best manuscripts of Mark did not contain Mark 16:9-20. And the long ending also contains some words and expressions that are not written in Mark's usual style, which may indicate a different author. Some scholars suggest verse 8 does not flow naturally into verse 9, which introduces *"Mary Magdalene, from whom he had cast out seven demons,"* as though she was not already mentioned earlier in Mark 16:1.[1]

However, in any case, the Good News is clear: *"He has risen"* (Mark 16:6)! It's possible Mark intended to write more but was prevented from finishing his narrative, or perhaps he wrote a longer ending that got lost or accidentally torn off the codex (manuscript). The prevailing view is that Mark composed an abrupt ending intentionally, which would be consistent with his short and quick writing style. And if we consider Mark 16:8 to be the end of Mark's Gospel, there is also a lingering, contemplative effect: The reader knows Jesus has been raised and is left to ponder what it all means.[2]

One scholar points out that the "open ending" of Mark serves to indicate to the reader that the gospel story is not complete — it continues on in our own lives as we receive the news of Jesus' resurrection just like the women at His tomb.[3] Every day, the tomb is still empty. And every day, we get to decide for ourselves: Will we believe, go, and tell?

WEEK 7

WEEKEND REFLECTION

& PRAYER

A REPENTANT HEART

If you have ever lived near someone who owned chickens, you're probably familiar with the annoyance of a rooster's early-morning crow. But imagine how Peter felt when he heard the rooster crow in Mark 14:68. He wasn't annoyed — he was ashamed and terrified. Peter had reached rock bottom. He had heard Jesus warn that "*whoever is ashamed of me and of my words ... of him will the Son of Man also be ashamed*" (Mark 8:38) and that "*whoever would save his life will lose it*" (Mark 8:35). Yet under pressure, Peter buckled and denied even knowing Jesus. He must have wondered if he had traded his eternal soul to extend his temporal life.

While we cannot know exactly what Peter was thinking, we can presume his heart was grieved toward repentance in some way because Mark 14:72 tells us, "*He broke down and wept.*"

But unlike Judas' story of betrayal (Matthew 27:3-10), Peter's is not a one-act tragedy. His repentant heart was met with Christ's forgiveness. We see a hint of this in Mark 16:7 with its mention of "*his disciples **and Peter***" (emphasis added), and John 21 tells us more about how Jesus gave this once-cowering disciple a second chance to become a Spirit-filled apostle and preacher of the gospel.

Like Peter, we all fail at times. But none of us have fallen so far that we are beyond the reach of Jesus' forgiveness and grace. Even if we've fallen into sin, ignored Scripture, conformed to the world, stayed silent about our faith, neglected prayer and dependence on God, lost our way, or carried the shame of our past for too long ... **God is not done yet.** Mark's Gospel shows us Jesus is the One who never lets us go. He wants to forgive us and break off all the shackles so we might become faithful, Spirit-filled believers who boldly live by His Word.

PRAYER

Heavenly Father, I know I am not a perfect person. I have failed many times, bent under the pressures of this world, disobeyed Your Word, and neglected to make Your Kingdom my first priority. Lord, I repent of my sins, and I trust that You are faithful to forgive. Thank You for Your mercy and grace. Please help me to walk daily by Your grace through faith in Jesus, in accordance with Your Word. In Jesus' name, amen.

NOTES

NOTES

ABOUT THE AUTHOR

FELICIA CAID SMITH

Felicia Caid Smith is a writer, speaker, and unapologetic Bible nerd. With a master's in theological studies and a graduate certificate in Greek studies, her greatest passion is helping women grow in their understanding of God's Word. Felicia has written biblical teachings for the First 5 app since 2024 with Proverbs 31 Ministries.

She also hosts the *Theology and Grace* podcast, where she dives into the intersection of theology and real life. She lives in north Georgia with her husband, and together they rely on Jesus (and coffee) to keep up with the adventures of their two sons.

Follow along at feliciacaidsmith.com.

ENDNOTES

WHAT KIND OF BOOK IS MARK?

1. Duvall, J. Scott and J. Daniel Hayes. *Grasping God's Word.* Grand Rapids, MI: Zondervan, 2012, p. 270.
2. Tenney, Merrill C. *New Testament Survey*. Grand Rapids, MI: Eerdmans, 1985, pp. 138-139.
3. Garland, David E. *The NIV Application Commentary: Mark*. Grand Rapids, MI: Zondervan, 1996, p. 19.
4. Lane, William L. *The New International Commentary on the New Testament: The Gospel of Mark.* Grand Rapids, MI: Eerdmans Publishing, 1974, p. 2.
5. Duvall, J. Scott and J. Daniel Hayes. *Grasping God's Word.* Grand Rapids, MI: Zondervan, 2012, p. 273.
6. Keener, Craig. *The IVP Bible Background Commentary: New Testament.* Downers Grove, IL: InterVarsity Press, 2014, p. 42.
7. Duvall, J. Scott and J. Daniel Hayes. *Grasping God's Word.* Grand Rapids, MI: Zondervan, 2012, pp. 287-288.

WHO WROTE THE GOSPEL OF MARK?

1. Strauss, Mark L. *Mark: Exegetical Commentary on the New Testament.* Zondervan Academic, 2014, p. 28.
2. Carson D.A. and Douglas J. Moo. *An Introduction to the New Testament.* Grand Rapids, MI: Zondervan, 2005, p. 172.
3. Strauss, Mark L. *Mark: Exegetical Commentary on the New Testament.* Zondervan Academic, 2014, pp. 28-29.
4. Carson D.A. and Douglas J. Moo. *An Introduction to the New Testament.* Grand Rapids, MI: Zondervan, 2005, pp. 172-173.
5. Tenney, Merrill C. *New Testament Survey*. Grand Rapids, MI: Eerdmans, 1985, pp. 160-161.
6. Ibid.
7. Lane, William L. *The New International Commentary on the New Testament: The Gospel of Mark.* Grand Rapids, MI: Eerdmans Publishing, 1974, p. 10.
8. Tenney, Merrill C. *New Testament Survey.* Grand Rapids, MI: Eerdmans, 1985, pp. 170-171.

WHEN AND WHY WAS THE GOSPEL OF MARK WRITTEN?

1. Keener, Craig. *The IVP Bible Background Commentary: New Testament.* Downers Grove, IL: InterVarsity Press, 2014, p. 39.
2. Schreiber, Lisa. "Inscribing Scripture on Your Child's Heart." Covenant Christian Academy, https://www.covenantchristian.net/inscribing-scripture-on-your-childs-heart.
3. Keener, Craig. *The IVP Bible Background Commentary: New Testament.* Downers Grove, IL: InterVarsity Press, 2014, p. 39.
4. Brooks, James A. *The New American Commentary: Mark*. Nashville, TN: B&H Publishing, 1991, p. 28.
5. Carson, D.A. and Douglas J. Moo. *An Introduction to the New Testament.* Grand Rapids, MI: Zondervan, 2005, p. 180.
6. Burge, Gary M. and Andrew E. Hill. *The Baker Illustrated Bible Commentary.* Grand Rapids, MI: Baker Books, 2012, p. 1007.
7. Lane, William L. *The New International Commentary on the New Testament: The Gospel of Mark.* Grand Rapids, MI: Eerdmans Publishing, 1974, p. 13.

8. Gonzalez, Justo. *History of Christianity: Volume 1.* Harper One, 2010, pp. 43-46.
9. *History of the Church*, Captivating History, 2021, p. 13.
10. Lane, William L. *The New International Commentary on the New Testament: The Gospel of Mark.* Grand Rapids, MI: Eerdmans Publishing, 1974, pp. 15-16.
11. Evans, Craig A. *Word Biblical Commentary 34B.* Zondervan, 1988, p. Lxxxvi-xciii.

WHAT ARE THE KEY THEMES IN THE GOSPEL OF MARK?

1. Lane, William L. *The New International Commentary on the New Testament: The Gospel of Mark.* Grand Rapids, MI: Eerdmans Publishing, 1974, pp. 1-2.
2. Garland, David E. *The NIV Application Commentary: Mark*. Grand Rapids, MI: Zondervan, 1996, p. 23.

DAY 1

1. Adler, Yonatan. "On the Origins of Tevilah (Ritual Immersion)." TheTorah.com, 2017, https://www.thetorah.com/article/on-the-origins-of-tevilah-ritual-immersion.
2. Keener, Craig. *The IVP Bible Background Commentary: New Testament.* Downers Grove, IL: InterVarsity Press, 2014, pp. 129-130.
3. Garland, David E. *The NIV Application Commentary: Mark*. Grand Rapids, MI: Zondervan, 1996, p. 43.

DAY 2

1. Keener, Craig. *The IVP Bible Background Commentary: New Testament.* Downers Grove, IL: InterVarsity Press, 2014, p. 130.
2. Brooks, James A. *The New American Commentary: Mark*. Nashville, TN: B&H Publishing, 1991, p. 43.

DAY 3

1. Wright, N.T. *Mark For Everyone.* Louisville, KY: Westminster John Knox Press, 2023, p. 9.
2. Garland, David E. *The NIV Application Commentary: Mark*. Grand Rapids, MI: Zondervan, 1996, p. 70.
3. Keener, Craig. *The IVP Bible Background Commentary: New Testament.* Downers Grove, IL: InterVarsity Press, 2014, p. 132.
4. Strauss, Mark L. *Mark: Exegetical Commentary on the New Testament.* Zondervan Academic, 2014, p. 111.

DAY 4

1. Keener, Craig. *The IVP Bible Background Commentary: New Testament.* Downers Grove, IL: InterVarsity Press, 2014, p. 133.
2. Lane, William L. *The New International Commentary on the New Testament: The Gospel of Mark.* Grand Rapids, MI: Eerdmans Publishing, 1974, p. 95.
3. Keener, Craig. *The IVP Bible Background Commentary: New Testament.* Downers Grove, IL: InterVarsity Press, 2014, p. 133.

DAY 5

1. Garland, David E. *The NIV Application Commentary: Mark*. Grand Rapids, MI: Zondervan, 1996, p. 103.
2. Lane, William L. *The New International Commentary on the New Testament: The Gospel of Mark.* Grand Rapids, MI: Eerdmans Publishing, 1974, pp. 101-102.

3. Strauss, Mark L. *Mark: Exegetical Commentary on the New Testament.* Zondervan Academic, 2014, p. 130.
4. Ibid.
5. Ibid.
6. Douglas, J.D. and Merrill C. Tenney. *Zondervan Illustrated Bible Dictionary.* Grand Rapids, MI: Zondervan, 2011, pp. 1117-1118.
7. Strauss, Mark L. *Mark: Exegetical Commentary on the New Testament.* Zondervan Academic, 2014, p. 131.
8. Ibid. pp. 140-141.

WEEK 1 WEEKEND REFLECTION AND PRAYER

1. Elliot, Jim. *Shadow of the Almighty: The Life and Testament of Jim Elliot.* Edited by Elisabeth Elliot, San Francisco, CA: Harper & Row, 1958.

DAY 6

1. Douglas, J.D. and Merrill C. Tenney. *Zondervan Illustrated Bible Dictionary.* Grand Rapids, MI: Zondervan, 2011, pp. 1258-1259.
2. Keener, Craig. *The IVP Bible Background Commentary: New Testament.* Downers Grove, IL: InterVarsity Press, 2014, pp. 135-136.
3. Douglas, J.D. and Merrill C. Tenney. *Zondervan Illustrated Bible Dictionary.* Grand Rapids, MI: Zondervan, 2011, p. 1259.
4. Keener, Craig. *The IVP Bible Background Commentary: New Testament.* Downers Grove, IL: InterVarsity Press, 2014, p. 135.
5. Bruce, F.F. *New International Bible Commentary.* Grand Rapids, MI: Zondervan, 1979, p. 1160.

DAY 7

1. Lane, William L. *The New International Commentary on the New Testament: The Gospel of Mark.* Grand Rapids, MI: Eerdmans Publishing, 1974, p. 139.
2. Ibid.
3. Garland, David E. *The NIV Application Commentary: Mark.* Grand Rapids, MI: Zondervan, 1996, pp. 130-131.
4. Strauss, Mark L. *Mark: Exegetical Commentary on the New Testament.* Zondervan Academic, 2014, p. 127.
5. Lane, William L. *The New International Commentary on the New Testament: The Gospel of Mark.* Grand Rapids, MI: Eerdmans Publishing, 1974, pp. 141-143.
6. Bruce, F.F. *New International Bible Commentary.* Grand Rapids, MI: Zondervan, 1979, p. 1160.

DAY 8

1. Douglas, J.D. and Merrill C. Tenney. *Zondervan Illustrated Bible Dictionary.* Grand Rapids, MI: Zondervan, 2011, p. 1073.
2. Burge, Gary M. and Andrew E. Hill. *The Baker Illustrated Bible Commentary.* Grand Rapids, MI: Baker Books, 2012, pp. 1017-1018.
3. Strauss, Mark L. *Mark: Exegetical Commentary on the New Testament.* Zondervan Academic, 2014, p. 184.
4. Ibid. p. 181.
5. Bruce, F.F. *New International Bible Commentary.* Grand Rapids, MI: Zondervan, 1979, p. 1161.
6. Strauss, Mark L. *Mark: Exegetical Commentary on the New Testament.* Zondervan Academic, 2014, p. 188.
7. Ibid.

DAY 9

1. Keener, Craig. *The IVP Bible Background Commentary: New Testament.* Downers Grove, IL: InterVarsity Press, 2014, p. 138.
2. Brooks, James A. *The New American Commentary: Mark.* Nashville, TN: B&H Publishing, 1991, p. 85.
3. Bruce, F.F. *New International Bible Commentary.* Grand Rapids, MI: Zondervan, 1979, p. 1162.
4. Strauss, Mark L. *Mark: Exegetical Commentary on the New Testament.* Zondervan Academic, 2014, p. 199.
5. Ibid. p. 200.
6. Ibid. p. 203.

DAY 10

1. Strauss, Mark L. *Mark: Exegetical Commentary on the New Testament.* Zondervan Academic, 2014, p. 216.
2. Ibid. p. 218.

UNCLEAN SPIRITS AND DEMON OPPRESSION

1. Garland, David E. *The NIV Application Commentary: Mark.* Grand Rapids, MI: Zondervan, 1996, p. 80.
2. Ibid. pp. 79-80.
3. Strauss, Mark L. *Mark: Exegetical Commentary on the New Testament.* Zondervan Academic, 2014, p. 96.

DAY 11

1. Keener, Craig. *The IVP Bible Background Commentary: New Testament.* Downers Grove, IL: InterVarsity Press, 2014, p. 141.
2. Brooks, James A. *The New American Commentary: Mark.* Nashville, TN: B&H Publishing, 1991, p. 96.

DAY 12

1. Lane, William L. *The New International Commentary on the New Testament: The Gospel of Mark.* Grand Rapids, MI: Eerdmans Publishing, 1974, p. 201.
2. Brooks, James A. *The New American Commentary: Mark.* Nashville, TN: B&H Publishing, 1991, p. 98.

DAY 13

1. Brooks, James A. *The New American Commentary: Mark.* Nashville, TN: B&H Publishing, 1991, pp. 104-105.
2. Lane, William L. *The New International Commentary on the New Testament: The Gospel of Mark.* Grand Rapids, MI: Eerdmans Publishing, 1974, p. 221.
3. Keener, Craig. *The IVP Bible Background Commentary: New Testament.* Downers Grove, IL: InterVarsity Press, 2014, p. 144.

COMPARE AND CONTRAST: JOHN AND JESUS

1. Strauss, Mark L. *Mark: Exegetical Commentary on the New Testament.* Zondervan Academic, 2014, p. 267.

DAY 14

1. Strauss, Mark L. *Mark: Exegetical Commentary on the New Testament.* Zondervan Academic, 2014, p. 264.

DAY 15

1. Brooks, James A. *The New American Commentary: Mark.* Nashville, TN: B&H Publishing, 1991, p. 113.
2. Burge, Gary M. and Andrew E. Hill. *The Baker Illustrated Bible Commentary.* Grand Rapids, MI: Baker Books, 2012, p. 1026.
3. Brooks, James A. *The New American Commentary: Mark.* Nashville, TN: B&H Publishing, 1991, p. 114.
4. Burge, Gary M. and Andrew E. Hill. *The Baker Illustrated Bible Commentary.* Grand Rapids, MI: Baker Books, 2012, p. 1026.
5. Ibid.

DAY 16

1. Garland, David E. *The NIV Application Commentary: Mark.* Grand Rapids, MI: Zondervan, 1996, pp. 284-285.
2. Strauss, Mark L. *Mark: Exegetical Commentary on the New Testament.* Zondervan Academic, 2014, pp. 312-313.
3. Lane, William L. *The New International Commentary on the New Testament: The Gospel of Mark.* Grand Rapids, MI: Eerdmans Publishing, 1974, pp. 261-262.
4. Strauss, Mark L. *Mark: Exegetical Commentary on the New Testament.* Zondervan Academic, 2014, pp. 312-313.
5. Garland, David E. *The NIV Application Commentary: Mark.* Grand Rapids, MI: Zondervan, 1996, pp. 289-290.
6. Strauss, Mark L. *Mark: Exegetical Commentary on the New Testament.* Zondervan Academic, 2014, p. 325.

THE "ALREADY AND NOT YET" KINGDOM OF GOD

1. Morgan, Christopher W. *Christian Theology: The Biblical Story and Our Faith.* Nashville, TN: B&H Publishing, 2020, p. 506.
2. Seitz, Collin. "The Word and Works of the Gospel," *For Christ, City, & Culture.* https://cseitz.weebly.com/blog/category/all. Adapted from patheos.com/blogs/paperbacktheology.

DAY 17

1. Strauss, Mark L. *Mark: Exegetical Commentary on the New Testament.* Zondervan Academic, 2014, pp. 330-333.
2. Lane, William L. *The New International Commentary on the New Testament: The Gospel of Mark.* Grand Rapids, MI: Eerdmans Publishing, 1974, p. 280.
3. Garland, David E. *The NIV Application Commentary: Mark.* Grand Rapids, MI: Zondervan, 1996, p. 310.
4. Ibid.
5. Ibid. p. 317.

DAY 18

1. Brooks, James A. *The New American Commentary: Mark.* Nashville, TN: B&H Publishing, 1991, p. 133.
2. Keener, Craig. *The IVP Bible Background Commentary: New Testament.* Downers Grove, IL: InterVarsity Press, 2014, p. 148.
3. Strauss, Mark L. *Mark: Exegetical Commentary on the New Testament.* Zondervan Academic, 2014, pp. 361-362.
4. Burge, Gary M. and Andrew E. Hill. *The Baker Illustrated Bible Commentary.* Grand Rapids, MI: Baker Books, 2012, p. 1030.

DAY 19

1. Garland, David E. *The NIV Application Commentary: Mark.* Grand Rapids, MI: Zondervan, 1996, pp. 329-330.
2. Brooks, James A. *The New American Commentary: Mark.* Nashville, TN: B&H Publishing, 1991, pp. 141-142.
3. Strauss, Mark L. *Mark: Exegetical Commentary on the New Testament.* Zondervan Academic, 2014, p. 385.
4. Brooks, James A. *The New American Commentary: Mark.* Nashville, TN: B&H Publishing, 1991, p. 143.

DAY 20

1. Brooks, James A. *The New American Commentary: Mark*. Nashville, TN: B&H Publishing, 1991, p. 147.
2. Strauss, Mark L. *Mark: Exegetical Commentary on the New Testament.* Zondervan Academic, 2014, pp. 398-399.
3. Ibid. pp. 400-401.

DAY 21

1. Strauss, Mark L. *Mark: Exegetical Commentary on the New Testament.* Zondervan Academic, 2014, pp. 407-408.
2. Garland, David E. *The NIV Application Commentary: Mark.* Grand Rapids, MI: Zondervan, 1996, p. 367.
3. Ibid. pp. 368-369.

DAY 22

1. Evans, Craig. *Word Biblical Commentary 34B.* Zondervan, 1988, p. 82.
2. Lane, William L. *The New International Commentary on the New Testament: The Gospel of Mark.* Grand Rapids, MI: Eerdmans Publishing, 1974, p. 353.
3. Keener, Craig. *The IVP Bible Background Commentary: New Testament.* Downers Grove, IL: InterVarsity Press, 2014, p. 93.
4. Brooks, James A. *The New American Commentary: Mark.* Nashville, TN: B&H Publishing, 1991, p. 158.
5. Ibid.
6. Lane, William L. *The New International Commentary on the New Testament: The Gospel of Mark.* Grand Rapids, MI: Eerdmans Publishing, 1974, p. 357.
7. Burge, Gary M. and Andrew E. Hill. *The Baker Illustrated Bible Commentary.* Grand Rapids, MI: Baker Books, 2012, pp. 1034-1035.

DAY 23

1. Brooks, James A. *The New American Commentary: Mark.* Nashville, TN: B&H Publishing, 1991, p. 162.

DAY 24

1. Garland, David E. *The NIV Application Commentary: Mark.* Grand Rapids, MI: Zondervan, 1996, p. 419.
2. Ibid. p. 421.
3. Strauss, Mark L. *Mark: Exegetical Commentary on the New Testament.* Zondervan Academic, 2014, p. 452.

DAY 25

1. "Passion." *Merriam-Webster's Dictionary,* https://www.merriam-webster.com/dictionary/passion.
2. Lane, William L. *The New International Commentary on the New Testament: The Gospel of Mark.* Grand Rapids, MI: Eerdmans Publishing, 1974, p. 393.
3. Ibid. p. 395.
4. Garland, David E. *The NIV Application Commentary: Mark.* Grand Rapids, MI: Zondervan, 1996, p. 428.
5. Evans, Craig. *Word Biblical Commentary 34B.* Zondervan, 1988, p. 147.
6. Garland, David E. *The NIV Application Commentary: Mark.* Grand Rapids, MI: Zondervan, 1996, pp. 428-429.
7. Lane, William L. *The New International Commentary on the New Testament: The Gospel of Mark.* Grand Rapids, MI: Eerdmans Publishing, 1974, p. 400.

A HOUSE OF PRAYER

1. Brooks, James A. *The New American Commentary: Mark.* Nashville, TN: B&H Publishing, 1991, p. 185.
2. Keener, Craig. *The IVP Bible Background Commentary: New Testament.* Downers Grove, IL: InterVarsity Press, 2014, p. 157.
3. Brooks, James A. *The New American Commentary: Mark.* Nashville, TN: B&H Publishing, 1991, p. 186.

DAY 26

1. Garland, David E. *The NIV Application Commentary: Mark.* Grand Rapids, MI: Zondervan, 1996, p. 452.
2. Keener, Craig. *The IVP Bible Background Commentary: New Testament.* Downers Grove, IL: InterVarsity Press, 2014, p. 159.
3. Strauss, Mark L. *Mark: Exegetical Commentary on the New Testament.* Zondervan Academic, 2014, pp. 531-532.
4. Ibid. pp. 534-535.
5. Douglas, J.D. and Merrill C. Tenney. *Zondervan Illustrated Bible Dictionary.* Grand Rapids, MI: Zondervan, 2011, pp. 1285-1286.

DAY 27

1. Burge, Gary M. and Andrew E. Hill. *The Baker Illustrated Bible Commentary.* Grand Rapids, MI: Baker Books, 2012, p. 1042.
2. Garland, David E. *The NIV Application Commentary: Mark.* Grand Rapids, MI: Zondervan, 1996, p. 476.
3. Ibid. p. 477.
4. Ibid. p. 478.
5. Strauss, Mark L. *Mark: Exegetical Commentary on the New Testament.* USA: Zondervan Academic, 2014, p. 558.
6. Garland, David E. *The NIV Application Commentary: Mark.* Grand Rapids, MI: Zondervan, 1996, p. 480.

DAY 28

1. Brooks, James A. *The New American Commentary: Mark.* Nashville, TN: B&H Publishing, 1991, pp. 184-185.
2. Strauss, Mark L. *Mark: Exegetical Commentary on the New Testament.* Zondervan Academic, 2014, p. 569.
3. Keener, Craig. *The IVP Bible Background Commentary: New Testament.* Downers Grove, IL: InterVarsity Press, 2014, p. 162.
4. Strauss, Mark L. *Mark: Exegetical Commentary on the New Testament.* Zondervan Academic, 2014, p. 575.

DAY 29

1. Brooks, James A. *The New American Commentary: Mark.* Nashville, TN: B&H Publishing, 1991, p. 212.
2. Strauss, Mark L. *Mark: Exegetical Commentary on the New Testament.* USA: Zondervan Academic, 2014, p. 578.
3. Coogan, Michael D. *The Oxford History of the Biblical World.* New York, NY: Oxford University Press, 1998, p. 437.
4. Strauss, Mark L. *Mark: Exegetical Commentary on the New Testament.* USA: Zondervan Academic, 2014, p. 579.
5. Lane, William L. *The New International Commentary on the New Testament: The Gospel of Mark.* Grand Rapids, MI: Eerdmans Publishing, 1974, p. 469.
6. Ibid.
7. Brooks, James A. *The New American Commentary: Mark.* Nashville, TN: B&H Publishing, 1991, p. 212.

8. Strauss, Mark L. *Mark: Exegetical Commentary on the New Testament.* USA: Zondervan Academic, 2014, p. 582.
9. Ibid. p. 589.

DAY 30

1. Garland, David E. *The NIV Application Commentary: Mark.* Grand Rapids, MI: Zondervan, 1996, p. 514.
2. Blomberg, Craig L. *The New American Commentary: Matthew.* Nashville, TN: B&H Publishing, 1992, p. 386.
3. Keener, Craig. *The IVP Bible Background Commentary: New Testament.* Downers Grove, IL: InterVarsity Press, 2014, p. 114.
4. Garland, David E. *The NIV Application Commentary: Mark.* Grand Rapids, MI: Zondervan, 1996, p. 516.
5. Brooks, James A. *The New American Commentary: Mark.* Nashville, TN: B&H Publishing, 1991, p. 222.
6. Garland, David E. *The NIV Application Commentary: Mark.* Grand Rapids, MI: Zondervan, 1996, p. 516.
7. Ibid. p. 528.

THE LORD'S SUPPER: FOUR CUPS AND A FUTURE CELEBRATION

1. Ferguson, Everett. *Backgrounds of Early Christianity.* Grand Rapids, MI: Eerdmans Publishing, 2003, p. 557.
2. Ibid. p. 558.
3. Ibid. pp. 556-558.
4. Ibid.
5. Keener, Craig. *The IVP Bible Background Commentary: New Testament.* Downers Grove, IL: InterVarsity Press, 2014, p. 115.
6. Blomberg, Craig L. *The New American Commentary: Matthew.* Nashville, TN: B&H Publishing, 1992, pp. 390-391.
7. Strauss, Mark L. *Mark: Exegetical Commentary on the New Testament.* Zondervan Academic, 2014, p. 625.

DAY 31

1. Evans, Craig. *Word Biblical Commentary 34B.* Zondervan, 1988, pp. 410, 418.
2. Brooks, James A. *The New American Commentary: Mark.* Nashville, TN: B&H Publishing, 1991, p. 234.
3. Strauss, Mark L. *Mark: Exegetical Commentary on the New Testament.* Zondervan Academic, 2014, p. 633.
4. Ibid. pp. 634, 638.
5. Ibid. pp. 638-639.

DAY 32

1. Brooks, James A. *The New American Commentary: Mark.* Nashville, TN: B&H Publishing, 1991, p. 240.
2. Lane, William L. *The New International Commentary on the New Testament: The Gospel of Mark.* Grand Rapids, MI: Eerdmans Publishing, 1974, p. 530.
3. Strauss, Mark L. *Mark: Exegetical Commentary on the New Testament.* Zondervan Academic, 2014, p. 656.
4. Garland, David E. *The NIV Application Commentary: Mark.* Grand Rapids, MI: Zondervan, 1996, pp. 564-565.

DAY 33

1. Strauss, Mark L. *Mark: Exegetical Commentary on the New Testament.* Zondervan Academic, 2014, p. 672.
2. Brooks, James A. *The New American Commentary: Mark.* Nashville, TN: B&H Publishing, 1991, p. 249.
3. Strauss, Mark L. *Mark: Exegetical Commentary on the New Testament.* Zondervan Academic, 2014, p. 675.

4. Garland, David E. *The NIV Application Commentary: Mark.* Grand Rapids, MI: Zondervan, 1996, p. 580.
5. Ibid. p. 586.
6. Ibid. p. 589.

DAY 34

1. Strauss, Mark L. *Mark: Exegetical Commentary on the New Testament.* USA: Zondervan Academic, 2014, p. 701.
2. Ibid. p. 702.
3. Ibid. p. 703.
4. Ibid. pp. 703-704.
5. "Posca." *Pass the Garum*, September 23, 2013. https://pass-the-garum.blogspot.com/2013/09/posca.html.
6. Strauss, Mark L. *Mark: Exegetical Commentary on the New Testament.* USA: Zondervan Academic, 2014, pp. 704-705.

DAY 35

1. Lane, William L. *The New International Commentary on the New Testament: The Gospel of Mark.* Grand Rapids, MI: Eerdmans Publishing, 1974, p. 585.
2. Keener, Craig. *The IVP Bible Background Commentary: New Testament.* Downers Grove, IL: InterVarsity Press, 2014, pp. 174-175.
3. Brooks, James A. *The New American Commentary: Mark.* Nashville, TN: B&H Publishing, 1991, p. 269.
4. Keener, Craig. *The IVP Bible Background Commentary: New Testament.* Downers Grove, IL: InterVarsity Press, 2014, pp. 174-175.
5. Garland, David E. *The NIV Application Commentary: Mark.* Grand Rapids, MI: Zondervan, 1996, p. 613.

WHAT IS AUTHENTICALLY MARK?

1. Carson, D.A. and Douglas J. Moo. *An Introduction to the New Testament.* Grand Rapids, MI: Zondervan, 2005, p. 189.
2. Ibid.
3. Brooks, James A. *The New American Commentary: Mark.* Nashville, TN: B&H Publishing, 1991, p. 275.

ABOUT PROVERBS 31 MINISTRIES

She is clothed with strength and dignity;
she can laugh at the days to come.

PROVERBS 31:25

Proverbs 31 Ministries is a nondenominational, nonprofit Christian ministry that seeks to lead women into a personal relationship with Christ. With Proverbs 31:10-31 as a guide, Proverbs 31 Ministries reaches women in the middle of their busy days through free devotions, podcast episodes, speaking events, conferences, resources, and training in the call to write, speak and lead others.

We are real women offering real-life solutions to those striving to maintain life's balance, in spite of today's hectic pace and cultural pull away from godly principles.

Wherever a woman may be on her spiritual journey, Proverbs 31 Ministries exists to be a trusted friend who understands the challenges she faces and walks by her side, encouraging her as she walks toward the heart of God.

Visit us online today at proverbs31.org!

P31 PROVERBS 31 ministries